Healing Trauma God's Way

Copyright © 2021 by Timothy Lane All rights reserved.

All rights reserved. This book is protected by the copyright laws of the United States of America. This book may not be copied or reprinted for commercial gain or profit. The use of quotations or occasional page copying for personal or group study is permitted and encouraged. Permission will be granted upon request.

Unless otherwise identified, Scripture quotations are from the King James Version. Copyright © 1982 by Thomas Nelson, Inc. Used by permission. All rights reserved.

Holy Bible, New Living Translation copyright © 1996, 2004, 2007 by Tyndale House Foundation. Used by permission of Tyndale House Publishers Inc., Carol Stream, IL 60188. All rights reserved. New Living, NLT, and the New Living Translation logo are registered trademarks of Tyndale House Publishers.

To contact the author, please visit: www.GodTherapy.net

Contents

INTRODUCTION 1

CHAPTER 1
    The Trauma Epidemic in our Churches 9

CHAPTER 2
    Having Church vs Being the Church 19

CHAPTER 3
    What You Hide Cannot Heal 27

CHAPTER 4
    How Trauma Travels 41

CHAPTER 5
    When Trauma is Mishandled 47

CHAPTER 6
    The Relationship Between Wounds & Demons 53

CHAPTER 7
    The Impact of Trauma 59

CHAPTER 8
    Why It's Not God's Fault 108

CHAPTER 9
    Why the Devil is Not The Problem 118

CHAPTER 10
    How Christians Become Demonized 124

CHAPTER 11
    The Benefits & Limitations of Therapy 138

CHAPTER 12
    The Benefits & Limitations of the Church 142

CHAPTER 13

METHODS TO HEALING TRAUMA GOD'S WAY 153

CHAPTER 14

KEYS TO HEALING FROM YOUR PAST 185

CHAPTER 15

KEYS TO TURNING YOUR PAIN INTO PURPOSE 195

CHAPTER 16

FROM MISERY TO MINISTRY 209

ABOUT THE AUTHOR **212**

Introduction

Through my inner healing and deliverance counseling practice, I have lead thousands of sessions and received many testimonies of people who were healed from some of the worst cases. Here's one testimony of many:

> "Happy New Year! I had to express my immense gratefulness for you, Pastor Timothy Lane. I suffered from depression for thirty years. [I've] been in church for years. After having private sessions of inner healing and deliverance and taking the Inner Healing and Deliverance Training course, I am free! Never until now had I walked in this wholeness. I don't live in fear anymore. My heart has changed. I walk in boldness, authority, peace, and JOY, at a level I didn't know was possible. It has stirred up my gifts more! God Therapy: Inner Healing and Deliverance is priceless!
>
> [My] symptoms of depression are gone, and I learn to recognize when the enemy tries to bring it back to me. I am not going to cover depression by working too much or sleeping. I am no longer bound. I take all authority and walk in dominion through Christ Jesus! I am taking care of my home, cleaning, cooking, and baking! And I start my new job January 5th! I am believing God for what he has ahead! I stand on

Introduction

> *His word! I walk in preparation anticipating with excitement of what he said is coming!*
>
> *I was the woman at the well, but now this JOY is uncontainable! The evangelist is being birthed! This JOY! I MUST go run and tell everyone about Jesus! God bless you, Pastor Timothy Lane! God Therapy is such gift to the body of Christ for such a time as this!"*

Even though this woman attended church regularly, she didn't experience freedom in Church. She went outside her church and was delivered through my Christian counseling practice. Just like this woman, most Christians who attend church regularly never experience inner healing and deliverance. This is because many churches have limited the ministry of the gospel of Jesus Christ to just preaching. Jesus never meant for the church to consist of proclamation without demonstration. Just like laces come with the shoe, inner healing and deliverance is supposed to come with the preaching of the gospel.

> *"The Spirit of the Lord is upon me, because he hath anointed me to preach the gospel to the poor; he hath sent me to heal the brokenhearted, to preach deliverance to the captives, and recovering of sight to the blind, to set at liberty them that are bruised." (Luke 4:18)*

According to this scripture, the work of the Holy Spirit in believers' lives should be accompanied by healing and deliverance, not just preaching. If churches consist of just preaching and there is no healing and deliverance, the cross is not being fully represented. As a matter of fact, it is underrepresented. It is like buying the shoe without the laces. It is akin to purchasing a car with no tires.

I pastored a church in the inner city of Chicago located near one of the largest housing projects in Illinois. I remember as a senior pastor standing in the pulpit looking out into my congregation and then looking out the window into the community, and saying to God, "If preaching is all there is for me, I do not want to pastor anymore. People are sick, demonized, and afflicted with mental illness. If you do not use me in healing and deliverance, please take this position from me because I do not want it." Even though I was an awesome preacher, could quote scriptures, and deliver an exegesis studiously, there was something in me that was hungry for more. I realized that after the people finished "shouting" and commending me for my excellent sermon, there were a lot of them that were still bound. This was when I decided to practice the following scripture:

> *"And the people with one accord gave heed unto those things which Philip spake, hearing and seeing the miracles which he did. For unclean spirits, crying with loud voice, came out of many that were possessed with them: and many taken with palsies, and that were lame, were healed." (Acts 8:6-7)*

There was something within that caused me not to be satisfied with just preaching a good sermon. I became desperate and hungry to see a move of God like the Christians did in the book of Acts. I became hungry to minister the gospel like the apostles Paul and Peter. I was determined to seek God until I experienced people being set free and delivered from the torment in their minds.

> *"And these signs shall follow them that believe; in my name shall they cast out devils… they shall lay hands on the sick, and they shall recover." (Mark 16:17-18)*

Introduction

I grew tired of speaking but not seeing the scripture come alive in my ministry and my church. This was when I committed to coming to the church every day and praying for one hour. For years, I came to the church and cried out to God for more. I laid before God on the altar with tears in my eyes and begged him to heal, deliver, and set free. As I began doing that, I could feel something stirring within me and being birthed. My faith began to build, and the power of God began to push me from praying to going. I realized that what I was praying for I already had. All I needed to do was to put it into practice.

After my sermons, I began making altar calls and praying for the sick. I also committed to going out into the projects of Chicago and praying for the sick at least three to four times each week. Initially, nobody was getting healed. Then it was like a ripple effect. At first 30%, then 40%, and suddenly it was like heaven opened for me and 80% of the people I prayed for were healed.

I would drive around looking for people who were on crutches, jump out of the car, and pray for them. One time, an older lady was walking with crutches. I pulled up and jumped out of my vehicle. She probably thought I was going to rob her. I asked her if I could pray that God would heal her. She informed me that she suffered a stroke, and as a result, she could not walk normally and needed crutches. As I began to pray, the power of God came upon her, and she began to weep, cry, and praise God while moving her legs without crutches. Two police officers were watching, and one shared with me while I was praying for her, his toothache was healed!

This became a catalyst whereby the Holy Spirit began dealing with me about ministering inner healing and deliverance. People needed emotional and mental healing even more than they needed physical healing. I began to walk people through inner healing and deliverance, and surprisingly, demons began to manifest and come out of believers. I used my clinical experience as a therapist, ministry experience, and the Holy Spirit's revelations to develop an inner healing and deliverance model that I entitled *God Therapy*. *God Therapy* is a seven-step model that systematically brings freedom from inner wounds and demons. Unlike traditional deliverance methods that perform deliverance in a public setting, usually during a church service where demons are encouraged to manifest to make a show, *God Therapy* is a clinical, therapeutic approach to deliverance. I meet with clients one-on-one in a private space, whereby they complete assessments. Then I systematically walk them through addressing demonic legal rights and the wounds and trauma that the demons are connected to. I consistently execute deliverance last after addressing the inner wounds and demonic connections. In addition, it is an encounter-based method where instead of the client experiencing demons, they have encounters with Christ. To my surprise, demon spirits come out within minutes and with minimal manifestations. This differs from my experience growing up where deliverance consisted of three to four men holding the person while experiencing crazy manifestations and taking hours to cast a demon out of a person.

After seeing hundreds of clients, I noticed a pattern. My clients were powerfully freed and would have these amazing God encounters where they could feel, sense, or see Jesus touching them, healing them, and setting them free. Sometimes they recorded seeing angels or feeling Jesus right next to them during the sessions. There were sessions where the power of God was so heavy on them that they would weep or lay prostrate on the floor as Father God set them free and filled them with

Introduction

his presence. The word quickly spread through word of mouth, and Christians began coming to me and getting totally free. I realized that one of the main issues why Christians were so demonized was because of the unaddressed and unhealed trauma they experienced.

There are a great lack of resources and trained ministers in the Christian church that can bring healing to Christians impacted by trauma. Christians need to be educated about trauma and equipped with the proper tools to heal from trauma. This book is meant to serve that purpose. Through the power of God, psychospiritual education, and clinical techniques, you can be whole.

For reference, here is the 7-step *God Therapy Model* from my book *God Therapy*:

1. **Removing of Sin, Guilt, and Shame:**
   A person is freed from the power of sin and experiences the power of God's love and forgiveness.

2. **Removing Unforgiveness:**
   A person is walked through a process to forgive from the heart and receive inner healing and deliverance from heart wounds.

3. **Breaking Word Curses:**
   A person's partnership with word curses connected to negative speaking, thinking, or verbal abuse are broken, and blessings are released instead of curses.

4. **Removal of Generational Sins and Curses:** Generational curses are broken, generational spirits are cast out, and

generational blessings are released.

5. **Breaking Soul Ties:**

    Soul ties connected to people, places, or things are broken, and you're delivered from demonic spirits connected to soul ties.

6. **Healing Trauma and Grief:**

    A person is walked through a process that brings healing and deliverance from trauma and grief.

7. **Deliverance from Demons:**

    Any remaining demons that have not been addressed in the six steps are removed through a powerful deliverance prayer.

Introduction

Chapter 1

The Trauma Epidemic in our Churches

When I started my *God Therapy* practice, I was shocked at the unaddressed need for inner healing in the body of Christ. There is an epidemic of trauma in the Christian church. From lay members to ministry leaders to senior pastors, people flooded me for inner healing and deliverance. Most of them had one thing in common—trauma. Trauma does not discriminate. I have had Christian clients from various denominations, backgrounds, locations, economic statuses, and races. One thing they all had shared was that they were dealing with present struggles because of past pain. What was disturbing was that the healing they needed they could not receive from their church, so they came to me. I was overwhelmed by the number of people calling, texting, messaging, and walking up to me because of a desire to be healed from trauma.

Trauma is any emotional response to a painful event that can cause psychological, emotional, and spiritual damage. I have realized from ministering inner healing and deliverance to thousands of Christians that there are a lot of Christians who are demonized because they have been traumatized. Even though they have a relationship with Christ, they are still suffering emotional and mental damage from something that happened to them in their past. They are worshipping while wounded and dancing while damaged. Some use religion to cover up their pain, but trauma does not automatically heal when you become a Christian. Just like you can become a Christian and still be physically sick, you can be forgiven but not totally free from mental and emotional wounds. To heal, wounds must be attended to properly.

Even though you have a relationship with Christ, you can still be suffering emotional and mental damage from something that happened to you in your past. You can go through the religious formalities but not really be free.

You may have been born in dysfunction or abuse. You may have been molested or abandoned. You may have seen or experienced some traumatic events or lost loved ones close to you. But you don't have to remain wounded and live in a state of trauma. Trauma is one reason why as soon as you give your life to Jesus Christ, the Bible says, "You must be born again" (John 3:7). It does not matter your age. You can be twenty-five or eighty-five, but after you give your life to Jesus Christ, there must be a journey of rebirthing through the process of inner healing and deliverance. It must go beyond joining a church, attending new members' classes, and attending service every Sunday. There must be more than giving your tithes, becoming a part of a ministry team, or connect group. All of this is good, but it is not enough. When you become a Christian, your spirit becomes new, but old thoughts and wounds from your past unsaved life can be brought into your new saved life. You may try to ignore it, suppress it, or praise over it, but your mind, body, and emotions remember the traumatic things that happened. It may be in your subliminal psyche, but it's still there.

"You can be twenty-five or eighty-five, but after you give your life to Jesus Christ, there must be a journey of rebirthing through the process of inner healing and deliverance."

Eventually, it will show up in some dysfunctional way. Not only does trauma cause inner wounds, but it is possible to carry demons from your trauma into your Christian walk. You need to be free from your past so that you can live a victorious, joyous life in the present.

I have found that inner healing and deliverance are powerful models to heal trauma if done correctly. Not only does it address the damage, but it also addresses the demonic spirits that can enter your life because of trauma. Inner healing and deliverance is what a lot of Christian churches are missing.

The fact is, there is a plethora of unaddressed hurt in the church, and we are preaching over it, singing over it, speaking in tongues over it, and not really dealing with it. I believe one of the reasons is that churches and leaders are not equipped to deal with trauma. They attend seminary to learn how to exegete scripture but not how to heal. They can interpret Hebrew and Greek but cannot correctly cast out a demon. I am not knocking seminary because I have a degree in theology. I just want to raise the question, why is healing and deliverance not a part of the curriculum in many Christian schools? Most of Jesus's ministry was healing the sick and casting out devils. The real purpose of the church is not just to preach; it is to help hurting people. The church is supposed to mimic the ministry of Jesus.

> *"For even hereunto were ye called: because Christ also suffered for us, leaving us an example, that ye should follow his steps:" (1 Peter 2:21)*

According to this text, Christ is our example, and we should follow his steps. Jesus's ministry was not just about delivering a sermon and raising an offering. There is nothing wrong with this because preaching and financial support are essential components of the church structure. However, Jesus spent most of his ministry healing the sick and casting out devils. Before his public ministry, Jesus was clear about his ministry mission and focus, and this should be the focus of every ministry.

> *"And he came to Nazareth, where he had been brought up: and, as his custom was, he went into the synagogue on the sabbath day, and stood up for to read. And there was delivered unto him the book of the prophet Esaias. And when he had opened the book, he found the place where it was written, The Spirit of the Lord is upon me, because he hath anointed me to preach the gospel to the poor; he hath sent me to heal the brokenhearted, to preach deliverance to the captives, and recovering of sight to the blind, to set at liberty them that are bruised, To preach the acceptable year of the Lord. And he closed the book, and he gave it again to the minister, and sat down. And the eyes of all them that were in the synagogue were fastened on him. And he began to say unto them, This day is this scripture fulfilled in your ears." (Luke 4:16-21)*

As you can see, preaching, healing, and deliverance are all a part of the Christian ministry. You should not separate them; they should intertwine. It is imperative that leaders receive training in healing and deliverance. Jesus was the first exorcist and inner healer. You cannot ignore the numerous scriptures in the synoptic gospels that share stories of how Jesus cast out devils. Then in the book of Acts, the apostles continued to cast out demons. We must keep the ministry of healing and deliverance alive in our churches. Without it, people will remain broken, wounded, and demonized.

Churches will never be fully ready and equipped to address members' mental and emotional needs if they do not develop inner healing and deliverance ministries. I believe the Christian church can no longer hide the need to be trauma informed, trauma trained, and have ministries designed to heal those suffering from trauma. There are too many hurting people in our churches to ignore this need. For the body of Christ to be healthy, inner healing and deliverance cannot be excluded from our churches.

YOU CANNOT BE NEW IS CHRIST CARRYING OLD WOUNDS

"Therefore, if any man be in Christ, he is a new creature: old things have passed away; behold, all things are become new." (2 Corinthians 5:17)

Growing up in the church, I knew this scripture because it was ingrained in me by the older saints. I did not realize that I could not be entirely new in Christ carrying old wounds. I also did not know that the newness that this scripture is referring to is a process. I believed that as soon as you confessed Christ as your Lord and Savior, everything was immediately new and all the issues you dealt with in the past immediately dissipated. I was taught that if you are a Christian, you could not have a mental illness or be demonized. So instead of dealing with our issues and demons, many of us denied them and covered it up with praise, worship, holding positions, and wearing lovely attire to church.

The preacher's goal was to preach you into an emotional frenzy so that you can feel good. Most of us equated feeling good to being free, but you can go to church and feel good and still be in bondage. I eventually realized that even though my sins were forgiven, and I was anointed, I still had unresolved issues that needed to be addressed. Becoming new in Christ requires a journey of inner healing and deliverance. Old wounds must be healed, and you need to experience deliverance from demons that may have gained access to you because of the unfortunate things you have experienced.

You cannot walk in the newness that Christ has for you carrying old wounds. After salvation, there must be inner healing and deliverance. Most Christians are not aware of this and are not taught this, so they stop at salvation. When you stop at salvation and do not address your inner wounds and demons, you will find yourself saved but sad, angry, hurt, and broken. You will be a Christian but a dysfunctional Christian. You are saved but still suffering from the unaddressed trauma and pain. You have been delivered from sin but not delivered from demons connected to the sinful lifestyle you use to live or the trauma you have experienced growing up.

My life was not totally changed until I experienced inner healing and deliverance. I was able to tap into the real joy and peace that every Christian should have because of our relationship with Christ. I no longer had to pretend to be happy; I was smiling from the inside out. It is essentially important to understand that your happiness is connected to your healing. There is a level of joy that you will never reach until you get totally healed and set free. You will not experience the abundant life that God has for you if you do not experience total freedom.

Some Christians have become professionals at wearing the proverbial mask and concealing a less than pleasant reality. God has provided a remedy, so this should not be the case. It breaks my heart to hear the tragic stories from my Christian clients. Even though they were in church, held positions and things looked together externally, they were troubled and tormented internally. Some on the verge of a complete collapse. That is because some wounds are so deep that just saying a prayer or hearing a good sermon will not fix it. There are some wounds so severe that "naming it and claiming it" does not cure. Unfortunately, a lot of our churches are guilty of making people feel like if they high five enough people all their problems will go away.

I recall a client whose mother was raped, subsequently became pregnant with her, and had a mental breakdown. She also suffered from seizures, which are believed to have been triggered by the trauma. She was born in a psychiatric facility, and as a young child, placed on three medications. By the age of four, she was diagnosed with various disorders and medicated with Ritalin, Clonidine, and Cylert! In addition, she was diagnosed with having a learning disability and placed in special education classes.

My client was placed in the foster care system and was tossed around to seven different foster homes. By the age of fifteen, she was molested by her foster brother who pretended to be her friend to get close to her. Even though she contacted the Department of Children and Family Services, no one helped her. Her foster mother was more interested in protecting her son than helping her. At the age of sixteen, she ran away to escape the abuse and became homeless. She then moved in with her boyfriend who physically and verbally abused her. She shared stories with me of how he would beat her, choke her until she blacked out, and even put a gun in her mouth and threatened to kill her. These experiences resulted in her abusing alcohol, becoming promiscuous, violent, and having poor self-esteem. She shared with me that she would wake up early and drink until she passed out. At a young age, her child learned to make breakfast for himself because she was too hungover to do anything. Sometimes she would not wake up until 5:00 p.m. the next day. This was her way of self-medicating.

Eventually someone introduced her to Jesus Christ, and she became a Christian. After she gave her life to Jesus Christ, she had to go through a process of healing and deliverance. Even though she was saved, she still carried damage. She had a great deal of mental and emotional issues and was heavily demonized.

We had multiple inner healing and deliverance sessions. During her first session, a demon manifested, and she jumped up and violently punched the wall. There was another session where a demon manifested and began to laugh and violently hit the ground. She had demons of torment, depression, fear, anger, rage, murder, trauma, witchcraft, and many more. With each session, her mental, emotional, and spiritual disposition became better and better. It was amazing to see her transformational process through inner healing and deliverance. Currently, she is one of the nicest, brightest, caring, and gifted people I know. I had the pleasure of training her, and now that she is free, God is using her to minister healing, deliverance, and prophecy to others. Looking at her now, you cannot tell that she has been through any of that. Because of her healing and deliverance, she does not look like the trauma she has endured.

Chapter 2

Having Church vs Being the Church

There is a saying that I heard growing up that the church is a hospital, where the sick go to get healed. If so, then why are 3,700 churches closing every year. You rarely hear about hospitals going out of business. The reason why hospitals stay in business is that there are always sick people around. If there are sick people, the hospital remains relevant because they provide a remedy. I believe if churches indeed functioned like a spiritual hospital, where people can come and their wounds are treated, ministries will remain relevant, and so many churches would not close.

One of the problems is that a lot of churches focus on "having church" instead of being the church. "Having church" typically means that there's good music, good singing, people are shouting, and the preacher's sermon titillates your emotions more than your spirit. In many cases, if you asked a member after the service is over to recall the fundamental scripture of the message, they are unable to, but they will say, "We had church." It grieves me that some churches are more focused on getting people happy than getting people healed. People are being stimulated, but they are not being saved. Their lives are not really being changed through the price Jesus paid on the cross to deliver us from sin. Some churches preach the gospel but do not demonstrate the gospel. Apostle Paul, one of the pillars of the New Testament church, set the example for effective ministry:

"And my speech and my preaching was not with enticing words of man's wisdom, but in demonstration of the Spirit and of power: That your faith should not stand in the wisdom of men, but in the power of God."
(1 Corinthians 2:4-5)

My father was a senior pastor of a Pentecostal Holiness denomination. Growing up in the church, I was exposed to some great preaching. We had some of the most famous preachers in our denomination come to my church, and it was mesmerizing. I loved to watch them as they whooped and dramatically delivered the gospel message. When I was twenty- seven years old, my father passed and I became the senior pastor.

Based on my upbringing and what I was exposed to, I thought that preaching a good message was the scope of what pastoring was all about. I figured that if I wore a robe, executed a good sermon, and got people emotionally charged, I did my job. Monday through Friday, I scrutinized my sermon. On Saturdays, I came to the church by myself, stood in the pulpit, and preached my sermon to the pews to perfect my message. I wanted to make sure I had a catchy topic, an engaging introduction, inspiring three points, and a conclusion that would have people running around the church. On Sunday, I did not eat; I fasted until service was over because I wanted God to use me to preach the people out the pews. I measured success by how the members responded to my messages with an "amen" or a "hallelujah." If they stood up, then I figured I was doing something. If somebody started running or what we call "shouting," then that was when I felt I preached the best sermon ever. My interpretation of what pastoring was about was flawed.

My turning point came when I was offered a job as a mental health counselor in the same community where the church I pastored was located. This community was a housing project and considered one of the worst neighborhoods in Chicago. The community was inundated with drugs, broken homes, domestic violence, prostitution, gun violence… you name it, it was there. The impact on the people growing up in this type of home and community environment caused many mental health issues. Interestingly, as I began to take residents through therapy, I realized that my church members needed the same type of support. Many of them experienced the same trauma, and just because they were Christians, it did not make them exempt from crises. They were still negatively impacted by what trauma does to a person mentally and emotionally.

I began to understand that church had to be more than just a whoop, a holler, and singing and dancing. There had to be more to church than programs, mid-week Bible study, and connect groups. These things were necessary and served its purpose in my church, but this was not enough. Preaching and teaching is good and necessary, but there is a certain level of pain that a good message and an altar call cannot fix. Some people have actual mental health and emotional challenges, and they require a deeper level of ministry. People need more personal ministry to resolve their issues. Even though Jesus ministered to thousands, he took time to minister to people on an individual level. He ministered to a woman that was at a well who had relational problems. He ministered healing to a blind man named Bartimaeus. There was a man with legions of demons who was excommunicated from the community, and Jesus cast demons out of him, and he gained his sanity back.

> Preaching and teaching is good and necessary, but there is a certain level of pain that a good message and an altar call cannot fix.

Christians are oppressed by demons, crippled by trauma and they need more than just a good sermon, they need deliverance. When this revelation came to me, I was no longer content with bringing a Sunday morning sermon, laying hands, saying a prayer, and then sending people on their way. I was no longer content with my members coming to me after service telling me how good a sermon I preached was. I knew that there needed to be a deeper approach to ministry and helping God's people with their mental, emotional, and spiritual needs than just "having church." I began to pray and cry out to God to heal and set people free. I remember standing in the pulpit with tears in my eyes begging God to anoint me to bring healing to the worst cases.

Then I realized that God had already given me the tools; I just needed to use them. It was like when Moses and the children of Israel were trapped between Pharaoh's army and the Red Sea. Moses cried out to God, and God spoke to Moses and said, "What *is* that in your hand?" He said, "A rod" (Exodus 4:2). God then told Moses to use what was in his hand to part the Red Sea so the people could be delivered from Pharaoh. Sometimes, the thing that we are praying for, God has already given us the power and the tools to get it done. We must use what is in our hands.

The instant I realized the importance of inner healing and deliverance, I made it a part of my pastoral care ministry, discipleship class and preaching. It was available for any member who felt they needed it. Even during Sunday morning service, visitors were given guest cards to fill out, and one question was, "Are you interested in inner healing and deliverance." I was shocked that most of the visitors marked that they wanted to experience this ministry.

This ministry immediately became in high demand. Not only did I have new believers eager to go through inner healing and deliverance, but also people who were long-term members expressed a desire to get healed from unaddressed wounds. This became one of the core ministries of my church. Through it, my church began to grow, and new people began to join because they were hurting and what was attracting them was that they heard the news that there was a place that they could come to be healed.

> *Sometimes, the thing that we are praying for, God has already given us the power and the tools to get it done. We must use what is in our hands.*

After realizing the importance of therapy and deliverance, my quest began to incorporate everything I had learned and practiced so that people could be healed. While most people separated clinical therapy, inner healing, and deliverance, I decided that an effective approach would be to merge the three. I developed a healing model that would utilize clinical therapy, inner healing, and deliverance. Next, I developed a team, set office hours, and provided a private, safe space for my members to come for inner healing and deliverance. They did not have to worry about being judged or their business getting out. They did not have to be concerned about someone recording their deliverance on their camera phone and putting it on social media. They could put their religious guard down, open up about their secret struggles, and receive inner healing and deliverance. Some of them had been in church for years, held positions, and were plagued by mental and emotional illnesses that no one knew about.

Chapter 3

What You Hide Cannot Heal

We have a propensity to avoid or block out painful experiences. Also, our body naturally makes us numb to protect us from pain. When we do this, it does not mean that the pain is not there; we have just disconnected from it. You may feel like it is not harming you, but the truth is either you are lying to yourself, or you do not realize the impact that it has. Even though these types of mechanisms such as avoidance, numbing, dissociation, deflecting, or projecting help us cope momentarily, in the long term, it has detrimental effects on you and those around you.

Imagine driving your car without having any maintenance done. You do not get the oil changed, rotate your tires, change the fluids, or anything else. You also ignore all the signs. The check engine light is on, but you just keep driving pretending everything is fine. To assist with your delusion, you get the car washed and waxed. The car may look nice and shiny and clean on the outside, but it is breaking down on the inside. This is what a lot of people do, especially in church.

Everything looks well-coordinated and clean on the outside, but on the inside, there is a breakdown. Instead of pulling over and fixing the issue, we just keep driving. Eventually, what is on the inside will show up on the outside. It will show up in your ministry, marriage, family, and in other areas. It could be a mental, emotional, or even a physical breakdown, but eventually the breakdown will happen. Unaddressed, suppressed pain from your past will always adversely show up in your present. Often, the trauma shows up subconsciously, which means you do not realize your actions, decisions, or reactions are connected to a traumatic event from your past. I always try to tell people not to wait until they crash to get help. Early intervention is the best intervention. The longer you wait, the worse it can get and the more damage it will cause you and those around you.

IN ORDER TO HEAL YOU HAVE TO BE REAL

The two primary steps to beginning the healing process are honesty and openness. What you hide cannot heal. You must acknowledge that what happened to you was traumatic. If you identify an issue, you can take the steps required to get the appropriate resource or support you need. Sometimes religion can stop us from being honest with where we are. Jesus told a parable of a religious man who could not get help because he used his religion to hide his issue. Then it shifts to a non-religious tax collector who was honest before God and forgiven while the religious person was rejected.

> *"Two men went up into the temple to pray; the one a Pharisee, and the other a publican. The Pharisee stood and prayed thus with himself, God, I thank thee, that I am not as other men are, extortioners, unjust, adulterers, or even as this publican. I fast twice in the week, I give tithes of all that I possess. And the publican, standing afar off, would not lift up so much as his eyes unto heaven, but smote upon his breast, saying, God be merciful to me a sinner. I tell you, this man went down to his house justified rather than the other: for every one that exalteth himself shall be abased; and he that humbleth himself shall be exalted." (Luke 18:10-14)*

> Unaddressed, suppressed pain from your past will always adversely show up in your present. . . . do not wait until you crash to get help. Early intervention is the best intervention.

I had a client whose father left her when she was two years old. She sat across from me with a flat look on her face and explained to me that it did not affect her. This was the lie she was telling herself to cope with the pain of growing up without a father. She convinced herself that this was not traumatic, and she was not affected. As I glanced at her mental health assessment, it told me a different story. It revealed that she was having severe symptoms of depression, angry outbursts, anxiety, difficulty sleeping, and a bunch of other things. What was happening was her suppressed pain was coming out in different ways. The hurt that she was stuffing was surfacing as symptoms.

I realized the first step to her being healed was for her to be honest with the impact of the trauma and allow herself to release the suppressed pain and feelings. I used psychodrama to assist her with digging into her subconscious and unlocking those blocked areas where the pain was stored. I had her close her eyes, picture herself at the age of two, and then picture her dad in front of her. Then I asked her to speak to her dad as the two-year-old girl and tell him what he did to hurt her. Finally, I asked her what she felt or sensed as she spoke to her father. Confidently she said, "Nothing," but tears were running down her face. Even with the tears, she was still trying to convince herself that there was no pain. What she did was become emotionally detached, and her coping mechanism was to stay out of her feelings.

The danger of this was that she became emotionally disconnected from her past and became emotionally detached from herself and her present relationships. She lacked intimacy in her relationship with God, her daughter, her husband, and others. Ultimately, she was able to be honest with the fact that she was still hurting from what happened, and I was able to walk her through healing and deliverance.

HOW PRIDE GETS IN THE WAY

The passage in Luke further reveals to us that the religious person had too much pride in his heart, and it hindered him from being honest about his issues. Also, God refused to help him because the Bible says God resists the proud (James 4:6b). Some of the most challenging people to minister to are those with pride. Even though they may act like they are perfect, they are usually the ones with the most issues. Pride is self-deception. It makes you think you're something that you're not. The Bible says this:

> *"For I say, through the grace given unto me, to every man that is among you, not to think of himself more highly than he ought to think. (Romans 12:3)*

The first-person Satan tricked was not Eve in the Garden—it was himself while he was in heaven.

> *"How art thou fallen from heaven, O Lucifer, son of the morning! how art thou cut down to the ground, which didst weaken the nations! For thou hast said in thine heart, I will ascend into heaven, I will exalt my throne above the stars of God: I will sit also upon the mount of the congregation, in the sides of the north: I will ascend above the heights of the clouds; I will be like the most High. Yet thou shalt be brought down to hell, to the sides of the pit." (Isaiah 14:12-15)*

Lucifer's self-deception lead him down a path of self-destruction. Arrogance keeps you in bondage, but humility opens you up to get healed. A part of humbling yourself is admitting you have a problem. You may have a title, you may be popular, and you may have many possessions, but you, too, have issues. You will never get the healing and deliverance you need until you humble yourself.

The danger with pride is that the worse it gets, the more arrogant someone becomes as a defense to protect themselves from the reality that they are not all they think they are. The more you challenge them, the more they will lie to themselves or become angry at you for exposing who they really are. Nebuchadnezzar's pride caused him to lose his mind, lose his kingdom, and run into the woods acting like a wild animal. What do you have to lose to become humble so that you can get healed? What's so wonderful about God is that he is a merciful, loving God. When Nebuchadnezzar humbled himself, not only did God heal him, but he restored everything that he lost.

> *"The same hour was the thing fulfilled upon Nebuchadnezzar: and he was driven from men, and did eat grass as oxen, and his body was wet with the dew of heaven, till his hairs were grown like eagles' feathers, and his nails like birds' claws. And at the end of the days I Nebuchadnezzar lifted up mine eyes unto heaven, and mine understanding returned unto me, and I blessed the most High, and I praised and honoured him that liveth forever, whose dominion is an everlasting dominion, and his kingdom is from generation to generation: At the same time my reason returned unto me; and for the glory of my kingdom, mine honour and brightness returned unto me; and my counsellors and my lords sought unto me; and I was established in my kingdom, and excellent majesty was added unto me. Now I Nebuchadnezzar praise and extol and honour the King of heaven, all whose works are truth, and his ways judgment: and those that walk in pride he is able to abase." (Daniel 4:33-34, 36-37)*

Nebuchadnezzar was a leader who developed severe mental issues. Can you imagine the impact that it had on his kingdom and the people that depended on him for his leadership? The blessings of being a leader are the positive influence you have on so many people. On the other hand, the dangers of leadership are whatever you go through or experience harms those around you.

ARE YOU LEADING WHILE BLEEDING?

All of us are leaders in some capacity. You may be a parent, employee, entrepreneur, mentor, or serve in ministry. You are a leader. Leaders are not exempt from needing healing and deliverance. I believe leaders need it the most and are the most neglected. We can become so busy helping others that we are not getting the help we need. Leading while bleeding, in its simplest terms, means you are leading while never taking the time to deal with your mental and emotional conflict. When you don't give attention to the root of your pain, you're bleeding. If you don't deal with your personal demons, not only will you bleed, but you will bleed on others and unintentionally hurt them in the process.

I remember listening to a pastor's wife sharing her story about how her father molested her as a young girl. This had a traumatic effect on her. She gave her life to Christ, married a pastor, and God began to use her in the church, but she never addressed the issue. She said she was "busy working in ministry and not working on her healing." These unaddressed wounds began to show up in her personal life and even in the church. She realized that she could no longer hide behind a title or position and needed to get help.

Like this woman, far too often leaders are not addressing their issues but continue to lead while bleeding. They continue to lead while depressed, angry, grieving, and broken. Usually no one notices because leaders are good at concealing their problems, but their problems only worsen. With some leaders, the worse it gets, the more energy they put into covering it up. Eventually, it will reach its apex and that leader may end up harming him or herself or those around them.

There was a time where I had a group session with pastors and their wives. I was honored at their transparency as they shared the trauma from their past that was sabotaging them in the present. They talked openly about being molested and abused and how they presently struggle with porn, infidelity, and other issues. They spoke about struggles in their marriages and families due to unhealed wounds from their parents. They came to see me because they realized that they could no longer continue preaching, teaching, and prophesying in public but living a secret, dysfunctional life in private.

They could no longer put up a happy facade while they were broken and depressed on the inside. Walking them through inner healing and deliverance was one of the most powerful, amazing things I have experienced. As they got down on their knees and wept in the presence of God, Jesus showed up and began to heal and deliver them. Not only were some of them restored, but their marriages were restored too. One pastor shared with me that his marriage and ministry were saved because of inner healing and deliverance. Another first lady told me that she contemplated committing suicide but now feels free.

The issues that these couples were experiencing had one thing in common. The root cause was due to past trauma that they were never healed from. Them being leaders in the church had no merit because trauma is not impressed by titles nor does it give preferential treatment. They carried the impact of past trauma into their marriages, ministries, and families because they never dealt with it. Many times, people's current failures are connected to past pain. Their everyday decisions and actions are motivated by traumatic ordeals they have experienced from their past. Even though they are Christians, they do not measure up to the character of Christ.

One pastor came to see me because he struggled with prostitution, drugs, and suicidal ideations. This was rooted in unprocessed, unhealed wounds from his past. His position did not stop him from his dysfunctional behavior. There are a large number of leaders like this pastor. They may have different struggles, but the root is the same—they are not addressing their issues. They are leading while bleeding. They know who God created them to be, but they are not living up to it because they are still broken on the inside. They appear to be okay in public, but in private, they are struggling. Their anointing doesn't save them from their agony.

Yes, you can lead while bleeding; however, you must come to the place where you realize you must do the work to deal with your matters. I understand the challenge leaders face with getting the help they need. For leaders, especially in the church, silence has become safe because being weak is not welcomed. There is such a demand to measure up to people's expectation that you don't deal with your damage. People look to you for breakthrough so who do you go to when things are breaking down? As a leader, you can't talk to everyone, but there is someone that can help you. It's important to find a private safe space to be real and heal so that you can lead with integrity and longevity.

"If you don't deal with your personal damage, not only will you bleed, but you will bleed on others and unintentionally hurt them in the process."

HEALING FROM YOU PAST

> *"And Peter answered him and said, Lord, if it be thou, bid me come unto thee on the water. And he said, Come. And when Peter was come down out of the ship, he walked on the water, to go to Jesus. But when he saw the wind boisterous, he was afraid; and beginning to sink, he cried, saying, Lord, save me." (Matthew 14:28-31)*

It takes a strong person to be vulnerable and transparent and ask for help. It takes a strong person to face their struggle head-on so they can finally be at peace.

When Peter was sinking, he did not pretend that he could swim. He did not look at Jesus and say, "I'm okay, I'm good." He realized that he was in danger and his situation was beyond his capacity to handle. He exclaimed, "Lord save me!" If he did not seek help, he would have drowned. Some people believe that asking for help is weak. Seeking help does not mean you are weak; on the contrary, it means you are strong. Weak people run from their pain and pretend it does not exist. It takes a strong person to be vulnerable and transparent and ask for help. It takes a strong person to face their struggle head-on so they can finally be at peace.

Here are the three main reasons why you need to heal from your past:
1. So you can be functional in the present
2. So you can have healthy relationships
3. So that you can have a successful future

As discussed, most people's dysfunction is connected to pain from their past showing up in their present life. The wounds will show up in your personality, attitude, decisions, and behaviors. Often, it shows up when a person overreacts— the level of their reaction does not match the situation. Some do not recognize that it is a past wound showing up in the present, so they blame and lash out at others, destroying relationships. Tackling these matters will allow you to heal and have a functional present.

It is essential to heal from trauma so that you can have a successful future. There's a popular image circulating on the internet of a woman walking forward to her future, but she is carrying several pieces of luggage and other bags. On each piece of luggage, a different word is written— "fear," "shame," "trauma," "rape," "anger," "abuse," and "pain." She is trying to move forward, but she has so much unhealthy baggage from her past weighing her down. I can imagine her gait is slow and labored. She is trying to build her future without first dealing with her issues to lighten her load. She has set her future up for failure.

Jacob manipulated his brother into selling his birthright and then tricked his father into giving him his brother Esau's blessing. Afterward, he ran to escape and never addressed the problems from his past. Like many of us, Jacob assumed that it would just go away over time. Not only did his problems not go away, they became worse. Esau was building an army, and he promised himself that as soon as his father died, he would seek revenge. Jacob reached a point in his life where God would no longer allow him to run.

> *"Then the Lord said to Jacob, 'Go back to the land of your fathers and to your relatives, and I will be with you.'" (Genesis 31:3)*

God told Jacob to go back so that he could deal with his unaddressed issues with Esau. God knew if he did not deal with the problems from his past, they would destroy his future. Sometimes to move forward, you have to resolve what's backwards. Jacob wrestled with the angel and was able to experience transformation. His name was changed to Israel. Something happened inside of him before it happened outside of him. When he changed, his situation changed. He was able to reconcile with his brother and resolve the pain from the past. Most times, change must happen internally before it happens externally.

What makes inner healing so powerful is that even though you cannot change what happened in your past, you can heal from the wounds of your past! As soon as you recover, you can learn from it, grow from it, and help others heal. Your trauma becomes a tool that can be used to minister to others.

Chapter 4

How Trauma Travels

There is a saying that time heals. When dealing with trauma, time does not heal; time hides. Trauma travels through memory. Sometimes the longer something sits, the deeper it goes into your subconscious memory. The deeper it goes, the more damage it can do. Instead of being medicated, the pain becomes integrated into your personality, emotions, decisions, and psyche.

There are four areas of memory that trauma travels through. These areas are mental memory, emotional memory, somatic memory, and sensory memory.

MENTAL MEMORY

When it comes to painful memories, I have heard people say, "Just forget about it" or "Let it go." You cannot forget some things or just let go of them because they become ingrained in your memory. You can ignore it, suppress it, deny it, or dissociate from it, but you cannot forget about it. Remember, true healing is not about forgetting but about removing the pain that is connected to your traumatic memory. True healing happens when the traumatic memory is processed and the pain released and cured. Also, through revisiting the traumatic memory, you can develop a new meaning or a new perspective about what happened to you, which is another vital piece to the healing process.

After going through treatment, I have had clients who blamed themselves, then realized that what transpired was not their fault. I can recall a particular client whose aunt was sick and called him late at night because she felt like if she went to sleep, she would not wake up. The client stayed on the phone with her all through the night to keep her awake. My client became very tired at one point, and both he and his aunt fell asleep while still on the phone. When the client woke up, he discovered his aunt had died. This client blamed himself because he felt that if he hadn't fallen asleep, she would not have died. The pain connected to his memory caused so much guilt that the client attempted suicide. After revisiting the event therapeutically, the client realized that it was not his fault and appreciated that his aunt was not alone and was able to transition with him on the phone comforting her. He could grieve his aunt properly and release himself from the guilt that he was responsible for his aunt's death.

EMOTIONAL MEMORY

There are incidences that your emotions remember that your conscious mind does not. Your emotional memory starts as early as three months gestation. This means even though you may not have any psychological recollection, your emotions can recall the feeling connected to what happened to you. Whatever you don't resolve, you will relive through your emotions. These negative feelings of fear, anger, sadness, anxiety, shame, etc. become engrained in your emotions and stick with you until properly healed. Suppose your mother wanted to abort you, but you were not mentally aware. In that case, you may grow up with feelings of rejection and abandonment and not know the cause because it is in your emotional memory and not your mental memory.

During a session, there was a client that, with the help of the Holy Spirit, I was able to take her back into the emotional memory of her mother's womb. She could see herself in her mother's womb and began to feel the hurt, fear, and sadness her mother felt while carrying her. As the client described what she was feeling, she began to cry. How is this possible? It is possible because while she was in her mother's womb, everything her mother felt she felt, and her emotional memory still carried the pain. As an adult, she was carrying sadness and fear and did not know why. I was able to walk her through healing her inner child that was traumatized in her mother's womb and she was free from the fear and sadness she was carrying as an adult.

SOMATIC MEMORY

Our bodies remember the trauma and abuse quite literally. The body keeps the score. Some people carry trauma and terrifying events in their body memory and nervous system. This means that the pain of what happened to you can be housed in certain parts of your body. Some people have psychosomatic illnesses and are physically sick because of mental or emotional pain. For physical pain to be healed, they must experience mental and emotional healing.

I had a client who had fibroids which are tumors and abnormal tissue growth. They were so severe that she appeared to be pregnant. After her inner healing and deliverance session, which addressed her trauma, she sent me a message the next day through a social media network and said:

> *"I wanted to say something... I had fibroids... and I don't know this morning, it's smaller than before. I mean much smaller. I'm so happy! I praise God! Your ministry is so important."*

After her third session, I received another message:

> *"I feel so free! I know this: The fibroids have dissolved since the three therapy sessions. They were so big it was like I was pregnant, and the fibroids were hard and heavy. It was hard to walk around, and it was pressing on everything. After the second session it went down to half the size. I believe it's about a week now since the last of the sessions and it's down more... I am healed and it's manifesting in my health also. I am ready to receive all my happiness. It's such a big difference, and I'm in awe of what God has done through this ministry! I've been on cloud 9, thanking God every day since!"*

There are many more cases like these that as I ministered to a person's mental and emotional ailments, they were physically healed. The reason why you're not physically healed could be because the root of the issue may not be physical. Your physical healing can be connected to your mental and emotional healing. God's desire is not just to heal mentally and emotionally, God wants to do a complete work and heal physically. Jesus cares about your mental, emotional, and physical health.

SENSORY MEMORY

Sensory memory is in your five senses: sight, hearing, smell, touch, and taste. Your body can store the senses connected to a disturbing event that can trigger a traumatic response. You can be walking down the street and smell an aroma that will remind you of something that happened to you in the past. You will get triggered at that moment and become sad, angry, or agitated because of sensory memory. Army veterans who have PTSD (Post-Traumatic Stress Disorder) may hear a door slam or fireworks go off during 4th of July celebrations, and their startle response gets activated, and they will feel the same emotions they felt while they were in war. Inner healing is crucial because not only does it heal the wound but cures the triggers that are connected to the sensory memory. You know you are healed when the sensory triggers associated with your trauma are no longer there.

Chapter 5

When Trauma is Mishandled

It is essential to understand that something can be traumatic without you being traumatized. Traumatized is when the trauma has a long-term harmful impact. If you receive the proper support, nurture, and treatment, you can heal and recover from the trauma quickly so that you won't become traumatized. The longer you wait to address trauma, the worse it becomes and the more damage it causes.

There is also another issue, and that is when trauma is not appropriately handled. Examples of trauma not being handled properly are when someone only prays for you and does not walk you through the proper healing methods; telling someone to have faith and believe but not helping them heal; making someone feel that they are not saved because they have emotional and mental health issues; and thinking trauma is a demon and doing deliverance without addressing the wounds. A person can become demonized because of trauma, but trauma itself is not a demon.

"Just stop hurting." This is the counsel an older Christian woman gave to my client. When people don't understand that inner healing is a process and requires treatment, they give religious responses and clichés that only exacerbate the issue.

As a young Christian, being told that I should stop being depressed made me more depressed. Dealing with trauma in the wrong way can make a bad situation worse. Sadly, to say, most of the time in our community, culture, and even the church, trauma is mishandled. This is what makes trauma so traumatic.

In her fifties, a woman carried so much rejection because of how she was mishandled as a child after being molested. The severity of her pain was connected to not being supported at the time it happened. Instead of her family moving towards her and loving on her, they moved away from her. Instead of her feeling like an innocent victim, they made her feel like she was the problem. This caused her to live a life of isolation and fear. As I walked her through inner healing, she could feel Jesus loving her and validating her. Jesus was giving her what she needed as a child that she did not receive from her parents. By the end of the session, the presence of God was so heavy on her she could not move. I am happy that no matter how long the trauma has been there or how severe it is, Jesus can heal.

It is common for victims of molestation or rape to be mishandled or not handled at all. There are loads of cases that are not reported because the family covers it up or the victim does not feel safe enough to share it with the family or another person they trust. In 2 Samuel chapter 13, King David's daughter Tamar was raped by her half-brother Amnon. What intensified the trauma was what Absalom, Tamar's brother, instructed her to do:

> *"Her brother Absalom saw her and asked, "Is it true that Amnon has been with you? Well, my sister, keep quiet for now, since he is your brother. Don't you worry about it." So Tamar lived as a desolate woman in her brother Absalom's house." (2 Samuel 13:20)*

You can see that Tamar's brother gave her poor advice. He was hoping that if she kept quiet it would go away. Unfortunately, this was not handled properly, and the situation escalated to where it caused more damage to Tamar and her family. Amnon was murdered by his brother Absalom, Absalom tried to kill King David, who had to escape

When Trauma is Mishandled

for his life, and then Absalom was killed by King David's soldiers. Tamar lived in isolation and agony for the rest of her life. If the traumatic event was dealt with, the family could have healed and recovered.

Like in this text, especially with sexual trauma, victims are told to stay silent or are afraid to speak up. This is happening far too often in families and in churches. Situations are swept under the rug as if nothing ever happened. I believe one of the reasons is because the family or church is more concerned about the negative publicity. Or the family or church are afraid of the adverse impact if people found out. This becomes more important than getting the person the help they need so that they can heal. The fear of having stigmas placed on the victim's family becomes more important to the family than supporting the child molested or raped by an uncle, cousin, or even parent. The church being sued or losing its reputation and members supersede the victim getting the help they need. The thinking is that it must be kept secret so the ministry and family remains unblemished. This causes the victim to be shunned, isolated, and left to deal with the trauma themselves. In addition to what happened to them, this becomes even more devastating. In these cases, the predator gets protected while the victim gets rejected. The predator gets a pass, while the victim is, in some cases, persecuted.

The best way to handle any type of trauma is to rally around the victim and give them the love, support, and nurturing they need to heal. The victim needs therapy to work through the pain of the traumatic event.

I want to reiterate that not attending to trauma properly causes long-term damage. Whatever is covered up compounds. It gets worse with time, especially childhood wounds. What is not addressed in childhood you will carry into adulthood, and it will manifest consciously or subconsciously in every area of your life. It will manifest in your behavior, decisions, how you parent, your marriage, your career, and your ministry.

I am a firm believer in deliverance, and in my Christian counseling practice, I do it frequently. Deliverance is a powerful process if done correctly. Some issues are influenced by demons. Demonic spirits can negatively impact an individual mentally, emotionally, behaviorally, and physically. After deliverance has taken place, the symptoms that the demons were connected to are no longer there.

It is also important to understand that not all problems are demonic; sometimes, it is hurt and pain. I have witnessed where a person's mental and emotional damage was treated like a demon. There was a lot of screaming, yelling, and holding the person down to cast a demonic spirit out that was not there. This did nothing but retraumatize the person and cause more confusion and chaos.

I have had several clients come to me after going from deliverance ministry to deliverance ministry, having exorcism after exorcism attempting to get free. Immediately, I recognized that the issue was not a demon. The root of what the person was dealing with was a manifestation of trauma. I had a pastor in my inner healing and deliverance class that was so grateful to me. She stated that all she knew was deliverance and had no clue about internal wounds. After taking the course, she realized that she was mishandling some people by taking them through the dramatics of deliverance, but what they needed was a process to heal from their trauma.

When Trauma is Mishandled

It is imperative that churches are properly educated and equipped to minister to those suffering from trauma. If healing and deliverance doesn't happen in the church, people will be forced to look to the world for what Jesus has commissioned the church to do. I asked my Inner Healing and Deliverance Facebook group of over 1,000 people this question, " In your experience, is church a safe space where people can heal and be delivered? Why or why not?" Unfortunately, most said no. Based on their personal experiences, here are some of their answers:

"Safe space, no. I've found, the leadership and the pastor always gossip about whatever you come to them with. Never will I ever go to a church for counseling. I'll see a Christian therapist if I must."
-Mimi

"No... church in my experience is not a safe place for people to be healed and delivered. I had a personal bad experience."
-Sybil

"I've never found a church understanding of trauma and my need for deliverance."
-Paula

"Depends on the church, I would say most are likely not a safe space. Most I wouldn't even want them laying hands on me let alone going through deliverance or confiding in them. Have had demons transferred to me many times in the past that I had to boot out after service. Plus gossip, total lack of understanding in healing and deliverance etc."
-Grace

Chapter 6

The Relationship Between Wounds & Demons

There was an erroneous post that a pastor posted on Facebook stating, "Depression is a demon." Sadly to say, this post received over a thousand likes from Christians who agree. One of the biggest mistakes I have seen in the Christian world is treating a wound like a demon. There is a difference between a wound and a demon. There is a difference between a wound of depression and a spirit of depression. A wound is a negative emotion, and a demon is an evil being that exists in the spiritual world. Demons can cause, influence, or worsen a negative emotion, but it is not the emotion itself. A spirit of depression can cause or worsen depression, but it is not depression.

> *As believers, we are not to hold on to negative emotions. We can experience them, but we must decide to let them go so they do not fester.*

Emotional wounds need to be healed. Demonic spirits are attracted to negative emotions and can attach to negative emotions and create a stronghold. Just like rodents feed off junk, demon spirits feed off pain and negative emotions. Therefore, the Bible encourages us to release our pain by casting it on him and not allowing ourselves to worry. As believers, we are not to hold on to negative emotions. We can experience them, but we must decide to let them go so they do not fester.

> Demonic spirits need to be cast out. Emotional wounds need to be healed.

When we hold on to our wounds or negative emotions, it makes us vulnerable to becoming demonized with the evil spirit connected to that emotion. If someone has hurt you, forgiveness is the key to letting go. To *forgive* means you chose to release yourself from the negative feelings connected to what they did to you. Below are some scriptures to assist you with releasing negative emotions.

> *"Casting all your care upon him; for he careth for you." (1 Peter 5:7)*

> *"And his lord was wroth, and delivered him to the tormentors, till he should pay all that was due unto him. So likewise shall my heavenly Father do also unto you, if ye from your hearts forgive not every one his brother their trespasses." (Matthew 18:34-35)*

> *"Do not worry about anything; instead, pray about everything. Tell God what you need, and thank him for all he has done. Then you will experience God's peace, which exceeds anything we can understand. His peace will guard your hearts and minds as you live in Christ Jesus." (Philippians 4:6-7 NLT)*

We can conclude from these scriptures that whatever sits attracts demonic spirits. If believers allow sin, hurt, worry, or unforgiveness to sit (lay hold to and draw close), then demonic spirits will gain access. Matthew 18:34-35 lets us know that it is crucial that we live a lifestyle of forgiveness so that we will not open doors for tormenting spirits to enter. Philippians 4:7 declares that if we pray and not worry, the peace of God will protect our hearts and mind.

Carrying worry and stress is an indication that a person is not praying like they should and bringing their issues to Jesus. Being in God's presence brings peace. The more you pray and seek God, the more peace you will have. The Bible says the peace of God will keep your heart and mind. The question is, protect your heart and mind from what? I believe it is talking about demonic attacks and infiltration.

Some Christians are so demonized because they are not releasing negative emotions such as hurt, anger, sadness, guilt, shame, or regret. This also includes not addressing traumatic memories but allowing them to ruminate or become suppressed. Holding onto these emotions and memories is like letting food sit in the open. Eventually it will become moldy, rot, and inedible. These repressed, harrowing memories are never treated or processed and that is when the demonic insects come, reside, and feed off those memories.

> *Carrying worry and stress is an indication that a person is not praying like they should and bringing their issues to Jesus.*

I had a session where a woman and her twin brother were conceived out of adultery. Her mother took her shame, guilt, and anger out on her twin children by verbally and physically abusing them. She told my client things like, "I wish I aborted you." Her mother eventually abandoned them, and their grandmother raised her and her brother. Her brother became involved in a sinful lifestyle. She had a dream that her brother contracted AIDS and died. When she woke up, she told him that God was telling her through a dream to warn him that if he does not stop the sinful, perverted lifestyle, he will contract AIDS. He was upset with her and did not speak to her for three months. Three years later, he contracted HIV and eventually died from AIDS.

As she began to experience the pain, I encouraged her to press into the pain and allow herself to cry, scream, and say whatever she needed to say to her mother or brother. I informed her that there was no right or wrong response, but she needed to release the pain that was stuck in her body. I began to walk her through the process of releasing the suppressed pain, and suddenly, without doing deliverance, demonic spirits began to come out of her. She began vomiting profusely. So much that she filled two buckets. I asked her how she felt, and she stated that she felt good and relieved. She then explained that she never grieved the death of her twin brother.

This was not the first-time demonic spirits automatically came out of a client as I walked someone through releasing pain. Factually, it has become the norm. As stated, demons hide and feed off painful memories. As soon as the pain within the memories is expressed and released, the demon spirits lose their grip and are weakened. Doing deliverance becomes simple.

Chapter 7

The Impact of Trauma

Trauma is an emotional response to a terrible event or experience. Anytime a person is under emotional or mental distress, there is a root cause to it. People are the way they are for a reason. A critical component of inner healing is finding out the root cause of where the pain originated. You can call this the scene of the crime. There is a story behind every wound. I call this the event vs. the impact.

The Traumatic Event vs The Traumatic Impact:

Event	Impact
What happened to you	How it is affecting you
In the past	What you have carried into the present (depression, anger, fear, anxiety, relationship problems, demonization, etc.)
Cannot be changed	Can be changed
Does not need healing	Needs healing & deliverance

When you experience trauma, it can be beyond your mental or emotional capacity to cope and can cause long-term damage. God created our bodies with a natural capacity and resilience to self-heal. Physically, your body will repair itself within two to three weeks. However, bodily damage can be so severe that it is beyond our body's capacity to heal itself and requires more intensive care or even surgery. Just like physically, we have this same innate mental and emotional capacity to self-heal. But there are incidents in our lives that are so traumatic that even though the event is over, the effect is still there, and more intensive care and special attention are needed. You cannot just go on like everything will be alright because if you do not get the help you need, it will only worsen.

As a child, I was very energetic and used to always do daring and sometimes dangerous things like climb trees, capture snakes, hunt mice, and fight with my older brothers. Yes, fighting with my older brothers was dangerous. One day, I decided to do something different and go swimming in a creek. The creek was so dirty you could not see through the water. While under water, I felt a sting on my finger. When I came out of the water, I was stunned to see my pinky finger hanging. The only thing that was keeping it attached was a piece of my skin. My body did not have the capacity to heal itself. I had to be rushed to the emergency room, and a doctor had to sow my finger back on. If I did not receive immediate help, I would have lost my finger. Trauma is like this: the worst thing you can do with trauma is ignore it and not get immediate support. This will cause you to lose your joy, peace, and emotional equilibrium. Your capacity to enjoy life becomes sabotaged. Instead of appreciating the moments and blessings of your present, your life becomes consumed with the pain of your past.

DEALING WITH UNKNOWN TRAUMA

Some people have experienced horrendous events and are unaware that what they have encountered would be classified as traumatic. They were raised in a traumatic environment and because it was the only life they were exposed to, they viewed it as normal. Someone may say, "Daddy always drank and became violent, but that was just how things were growing up in our household." Just because something is familiar in our

The Impact of Trauma

community, family, religion, or sphere of influence does not mean it is okay.

As a kid growing up in church, it was customary for us (me and the other church kids) to get what we called "whippings" or "beatings." There were no rules to these whippings, anything and everything could be used as a weapon... I mean tool. We were whipped with hangers, belts, extension cords, sticks, shoes, or whatever else our parents could grab. No place on your body was off-limits. I believe I got hit on every area of my body. I think the worst beating, I mean spanking, was in the bathtub with an extension cord. This type of discipline was erroneously excused by scripture stating, *"He that spareth his rod hateth his son: but he that loveth him chasteneth him betimes"* (Proverbs 13:24).

Now I do believe that corporal punishment is biblical, but there is a line between properly disciplining your child physically and abuse. It was not until I was an adult that I realized that this was abuse and was detrimental to my mental and emotional health. I do not fault my parents because this was their cultural and religious norm. They were doing what they were taught was right even though it was wrong. The first step in addressing unknown trauma is to recognize what you have been through is traumatic. Once you realize it, you can heal from it and not pass it down to your children. That generational pattern of dysfunction will be broken through your healing.

There is a propensity to normalize what is abnormal due to it being culturally or religiously justified. If what you have experienced had a negative long-term effect on you, it is traumatic. If it is causing unwanted mental, emotional, and physical discomforts, that's trauma. You may need a therapist or someone familiar with trauma to make you aware that what you have experienced was traumatic. The next step is to get the proper support, counseling, or ministry so that you can get healed. When you become aware, it is your responsibility to seek help.

HOW TRAUMA AFFECTS YOUR IDENTITY

"And God said, Let us make man in our image, after our likeness:" (Genesis 1:26)

"I will praise thee; for I am fearfully and wonderfully made: marvellous are thy works; and that my soul knoweth right well." (Psalm 139:14)

You were created to be like Father God. According to the scriptures, he created you in his image and in his likeness.

In other words, God created you to be like him. He created you to be a person of love, joy, peace, goodness, and righteousness. You were not created to be bipolar, depressed, violent, immoral, impulsive, antisocial, or fearful. Your true self was created to be emotionally stable, have a positive self-image, and to be relationally functional. You were made to have a healthy self and a healthy social life. This is what your true self is, the person God created you to be.

Your false or damaged self is the person you have become because of what happened to you. You were not created dysfunctional. Something happened that interrupted God's divine programming of your mental and emotional state. This caused your true self to become damaged and your false self to emerge. It is important to understand that this person is not who you are. That part of you that you do not like or have done things that you are not proud of is not who you are. That part of you that is emotionally unstable or mentally tormented is not who you are. That part of you that lives a secret life or has hidden struggles no one knows about is not your true self. It is the effect or result of some trauma. Usually, you can trace it to its root.

The good news is because that is not who you are and who God created you to be, you can change, be healed, and be restored! In the Bible, Jacob really was not a trickster. He was just acting out of the word curse his mother placed on him when she named him Jacob, which means "trickster." From a child up until adulthood, everyone called him Jacob, which means supplanter or trickster. This was mentally and emotionally damaging for him. Once Father God changed his name and showed him who he was—Israel, a prince that has power with God—his true self emerged.

> *"And he said, Let me go, for the day breaketh. And he said, I will not let thee go, except thou bless me. And he said unto him, What is thy name? And he said, Jacob. And he said, Thy name shall be called no more Jacob, but Israel: for as a prince hast thou power with God and with men, and hast prevailed." (Genesis 32: 26-28)*

After you are healed from trauma, then your true self can arise and you can have a healthy relationship with yourself, God, and others. You will no longer act out of the pain from your past but from the image of your heavenly Father.

"

God created you to be like him. He created you to be a person of love, joy, peace, goodness, and righteousness.

"

What are the 6 Effects of Trauma

Normal Self		Damaged Self
True Self • Who God created you to be	**Trauma Hits** ➡ **Something Happens**	False Self • Who you became because of trauma
Emotionally Stable		Emotionally Imbalanced
Healthy Identity		Damaged Identity
Relationally Functional		Wounded Messages
Rational Belief System		Relationally Dysfunctional
		Demon Spirits Enter

Even though I was a Christian, I did not know who I was as a person until I got healed from depression. Once healed, it was a journey for me to learn who I was for the first time. I was relieved that the depressed me was not me. The person that stayed in the house, laid in the bed all day, did not want to be around people, and carried so many negative thoughts about himself was not me. After I was healed, the new me, or should I say, the real me began to develop which was the total opposite of my depressed false self. I fell in love with myself because I realized the person that I did not like was not me.

You can find happiness in understanding that the part of you that you do not like is not you! That part of you that made those mistakes or did those bad things is not who you are. That part of you that is full of hurt, anger, guilt, and shame is not you. It is the broken, damaged version of yourself. The beauty of inner healing is after you get healed, the real you can surface.

"God said, Let us make man in our image, after our likeness: and let them have dominion over the fish of the sea, and over the fowl of the air, and over the cattle, and over all the earth, and over every creeping thing that creepeth upon the earth. So God created man in his own image, in the image of God created he him; male and female created he them. And God blessed them, and God said unto them, Be fruitful, and multiply, and replenish the earth, and subdue it: and have dominion over the fish of the sea, and over the fowl of the air, and over every living thing that moveth upon the earth. And God saw everything that he had made, and, behold, it was very good." (Genesis 1:26-28; 31)

Anytime you wonder who you really are, just think of who God is. He is love, joy, peace, and happiness, and so are you. He is merciful, kind, patient, gentle, and strong, and so are you. You are blessed because he blessed you to be blessed. You have dominion because he gave it to you. He is a good God and he created you to be a good person. It doesn't matter what you have done, been diagnosed with, or have been labeled as, your creator has already predetermined your identity and authority. All you must do now is realize it, heal, and walk in it.

> *Anytime you wonder who you really are, just think of who God is. He is love, joy, peace, and happiness, and so are you. He is merciful, kind, patient, gentle, and strong, and so are you.*

It doesn't matter what the diagnosis is, what people say about you, or what you have done; don't accept that as who you are. Never give up on yourself. With God, change is possible. Keep pressing into your healing and deliverance. Many times, what has happened to people are not their fault, but they must fight to get the healing they need to be free. Many of the poor decisions people make or things that they do are them acting out of the trauma they experienced. They were born into dysfunction or became a victim to someone's abuse. You did not get yourself into it, but as an adult, you must get yourself out. As a child or adolescent, you didn't have the maturity, resources, and resilience to overcome. Now, as an adult, you can take your power back and get the healing you need. It may not be your fault but it's your fight.

TRAUMATIC DEFENSE PERSONALITIES

As a result of traumatic experiences, people can develop what I call traumatic defense personalities. These are coping mechanisms used to hide or protect a person from pain. There are several reasons these personalities are developed. It can result from their wounded self being too broken to function in their present reality, so they develop a false character. It could be for the purpose of hiding or coping with trauma, insecurity, fear, low-self-esteem, shame, or guilt. It can result from them not knowing who they are or not liking who they are, so they create an alternate character or ego. You become an actor, but there is no movie; it is your real life. The problem with traumatic defense personalities is they are usually dysfunctional because they are created from pain. Also, demons can become integrated into these personalities, and when you become triggered, it is not just the false you that materializes, it is a demonic spirit as well.

A severe case of this is diagnosed as Dissociative Identity Disorder (DID) in the DSM-5 (The Diagnostic and Statistical Manual of Mental Disorders). Dissociative Identity Disorder is associated with overwhelming experiences, traumatic events and abuse that occurred in childhood. It is the existence of two or more distinct identities (or "personality states"). Even though people may not have DID, they may have its symptoms in a milder form. The overall purpose of these traumatic defense personalities is to cover up or protect them from pain. Some rely on these defense personalities to survive their present turmoil. The issue is after the turmoil is over, the defense personality remains and can cause them to develop self-sabotaging behavior because what worked in a chaotic environment does not work in a healthy, normal environment. What helped you survive a chaotic childhood does not help you function as an average adult. What supported you to make it through an abusive relationship does not allow you to operate as a good husband or wife.

I had a client that dealt with domestic abuse, not only from her spouse but from her spouse's family that she lived with. Her true self was a calm, even-tempered, kind person. To survive her hostile environment, she developed an angry, violent, explosive personality. When she was triggered, it was reminiscent of the incredible hulk, and she destroyed everything around her. It worked because this caused her boyfriend and his family to withdraw from her. After all, they thought she lost her mind.

> What helped you to survive a chaotic childhood does not help you to function as a normal adult. What supported you to make it through an abusive relationship does not help you to operate as a good husband or wife.

She shared with me a memory of the family ganging up on her and her raging through the house, yelling that she would kill everybody inside. This caused them to leave her alone because they figured she was "crazy." She eventually got out of the situation, and years later, married the right person. Even though what she experienced was over, the incredible hulk was still there and causing chaos in her marriage. She would become easily triggered and hyper-aggressive. She was paranoid that her husband would treat her like her boyfriend, and the hulk would emerge to protect her and harm anything in its path. What worked in the chaos was not working in the calm after the chaos was over. To have a happy marriage, she had to get healing and deliverance from not only the hurt but the hulk.

Another example would be with people who are war veterans or incarcerated. To survive, some develop a violent personality. This assists them with accomplishing their mission while in battle or not being victimized in prison; however, when they return to normal society, this type of approach in dealing with people no longer works. The reality is while the traumatic defense personality can allow you to numb or hide to cope with the pain, it usually ends up causing more pain. Not only are you not addressing or healing from the past, but you also create more pain because of a maladaptive, inauthentic personality operating in your present.

Without inner healing and deliverance, these dysfunctional defense personalities remain. In addition to inner healing and deliverance, there must be a process of you getting to know your true healed self. Instead of acting out of dysfunction, learn healthy coping mechanisms. Tap into your identity in Christ to address your weaknesses and challenges in life. Only when this process is complete can your true self replace your false self.

Here are some examples of maladaptive defense personalities that can develop because of unhealed trauma and demonic bondage:

- **The Denier:** Says things like, "I'm good" or "It's okay," but are really suppressing hurt and avoiding issues.

- **The Intellectual:** Acting and talking intelligently to cover up insecurities and feelings of inadequacy.

- **The Macho Man:** Acting tough usually to cover up fear, insecurity and feeling of being inadequate.

- **The Addict:** Self-medicates pain through addictive behaviors such as eating, sex, drugs, shopping, etc. The real issue is never addressed which triggers the dependence to continue the addictive behavior.

- **The Hyper Spiritual:** Spiritually preoccupied and out of balance. Makes poor decisions and says that God told them to do it.

- **The Sensitive Person:** This person is emotionally raw. They are easily hurt, easily offended, and easily triggered. These people find it difficult to forgive and let go of things.

- **The Narcissist:** Everything is about them because they have rejection and abandonment issues. Most likely they did not get the attention they needed as a child, so they seek to be the center of attention as an adult.

- **The Materialist:** Reaches for things to fulfill a void. They are unhappy with themselves or their life, so they cover it up with things to create a false sense of happiness and fulfilment. May also deal with pride.

- **The Sabotager:** Gets in their own way. Their self-destructive behavior is connected to unhealed emotional pain. They are acting out because of the wounds inside of them.

- **The Loner:** Isolates, avoids, and withdraws to protect themselves from being hurt. Has a lot of pent-up, suppressed pain that eventually causes an explosion or implosion.

- **The Angry Person:** Uses anger to feel control and manipulate people and situations. Anger is a surface emotion. Underneath the anger, there is pain, fear, shame, grief, trauma, etc.

While I've listed these individually, it is important to know that a person can express more than one of these defense personalities simultaneously.

COGNITIVE DISTORTIONS

Trauma can cause a person to develop cognitive distortions. These are mentally dysfunctional patterns of thinking that ultimately impacts your mood, behavior, and may cause demonization. They are chronic errors of thinking that develop over time due to an adverse event that causes people to view reality in inaccurate, harmful ways.

Here is a list of common cognitive distortions:

- **Blaming**: This is when a person blames themselves others for what they are not responsible for. I have witnessed this with a lot of my clients who have childhood trauma. Children are usually ego-centric and do not have the mental capacity to understand that they were victims of something beyond their control. They blame themselves for what happened and carry that blame into their adult life.

- **Labeling:** This is when a person confuses their mistakes with their identity. Instead of saying, "I've failed," you tell yourself, "I am a failure." It is important to realize that what you did or what happened to you is not who you are. You must commit to identifying yourself, not by your crisis, but by what your Creator says about you.

    "But ye are a chosen generation, a royal priesthood, a holy nation, a peculiar people; that ye should shew forth the praises of him who hath called you out of darkness into his marvellous light: Which in time past were not a people, but are now the people of God: which had not obtained mercy, but now have obtained mercy." (1 Peter 2: 9-10)

- **Magnification or Minimizing:** Magnification is when an individual blows thing out of proportion. They exaggerate and thus exacerbate whatever situation they are dealing with. Socially, they make things much worse than what they really are. Minimizing is when a person does not accept the severity of a situation. They usually downplay their pain and trauma. An example is a person who is an alcoholic and minimizes that he has a drinking problem. You must accept the reality of the situation so that you can heal properly and get the appropriate support.

- **Spiritualizing:** This person is hyper-spiritual. Everything is either God or the devil. This can cause a person to blame God or demons for the events that happened in their life. They can't recover because they don't take responsibility. Everything is not a demon, and everything is not of God. Some things result from the decisions that we make in our lives or the choices and sins of the lives of those we grew up around which adversely impacted us. The fall of humanity was not because of the devil. Even though the serpent influenced Adam and Eve, they made a conscious decision to disobey God and eat from the fruit of the tree which they were commanded not to eat from. As a result of their bad choices, humankind was affected, and sin entered the world. Even if what happened to you is not your fault, change requires you to take responsibility and ownership to fix what is broken in you.

- **Projecting:** This is when people place their unhealthy emotions, desires, or thoughts onto someone else. An example of this would be a person expressing feeling like people do not like them when they do not like themselves. In this case, the individual must become aware of their projection, take ownership of it, trace where it is coming from, and receive inner healing and deliverance in that area.

- **Negative Cognitive Filter:** When someone focuses on the bad and ignores the good. They accept the negative and discount the positive. In order to heal, it is important to think about positive things that have happened and accept that life consists of the good and the bad.

- **All or Nothing Thinking**: Views life in black or white. Things are always this way or always that way. There is no gray or neutral area for them. In this case you must develop a balanced way of thinking and realize that there are some grey areas. You must recognize not all things are not always one way and identify the good in life.

- **Overgeneralization:** Generalizes isolated events in their life and makes them a pattern. An example is if this individual fails one test, then they believe they always fail. They accept the belief system that they are a failure. In other words, they take on the identity or label of what happened to them. You must learn not to label yourself based on isolated events. See yourself how God sees you and accept that just because you may fail doesn't mean you're a failure. Just because you have lost at something does not mean you are a loser. Stop labeling and learn to accept the lessons life gives you whether you lose or win.

- **Emotional Reasoning:** A belief system that if you feel it then it must be true: "I feel stupid, so I must be stupid" or "I feel like I can't make it so I must not be able to" or "I feel like a sinner so I must not be saved." You must understand and accept that the Bible says that we "walk by faith and not by sight" (2 Corinthians 5:7). You must renounce the negative labels and commit to trusting God's word despite how they feel.

- **Fortune-telling:** When a person jumps to conclusions and makes pessimistic predictions of what will happen. This person assumes that something terrible is going to happen in the future. It is important for this individual to examine the quality of their evidence for the prediction and to consider their previous track record when situations didn't go as badly as predicted.

There can be demonic spirits connected to these distortions. Demonic spirits use our trauma to speak lies to us about ourselves, which creates cognitive distortions. The Bible lets us know that the devil is the father of lies (John 8:44). When you accept and believe these messages, it opens you up to become not only wounded but demonized. You must replace the wounded messages with a healthy message. It is good practice to find scriptures you can utilize to combat any wounded messages you may be carrying.

FROM A HURT PLACE TO A HEALED PLACE

Trauma is like a tornado. What is sometimes more devastating than the actual event is the aftermath. There are several differences between the event and the impact. As stated previously, the event is what happens to you, it is in the past, and cannot be changed. The impact is how it is affecting you presently. You cannot heal from the event, but you can recover from its impact.

In 2 Samuel 4:4, we are introduced to a character named Mephibosheth. He was King Saul's grandson, who was dropped by his nurse at the age of five. This resulted in him becoming crippled in both of his feet. He is not dead, but crippled. Like Mephibosheth, some things may have happened in your life. It may not have killed you, but it has crippled you. You may not be crippled physically, but you have become disabled mentally, emotionally, and spiritually. Mephibosheth had a royal name called Merib-baal, but when he became disabled, his name was changed to Mephibosheth, which means shame. This is symbolic of how the impact of the event can cause wounds of shame. Mephibosheth carried the humiliation of being crippled and was embarrassed by what happened to him.

After the traumatic incident, his nurse takes him directly to a town called Lodebar where he lives for the next twenty years. The word "Lodebar" in Hebrew means an unpleasant place. Sometimes, our situations cause us to live in an unpleasant place. This may not be a physical place, but it causes us to live in a place of sadness, anger, doubt, fear, guilt, shame, grief, and demonization. Mephibosheth was an adult and still dealing with the impact of something that happened twenty years ago. I am so glad that this is not the end of his story. King David sends for him and calls him out of Lodebar and does three things for him: shows him kindness, restores him, and allows him to eat bread at the King's table.

> *"And David said unto him, Fear not: for I will surely shew thee kindness for Jonathan thy father's sake, and will restore thee all the land of Saul thy father; and thou shalt eat bread at my table continually." (2 Samuel 9:7)*

The Bible tells us to "taste and see that the Lord is good" (Psalm 34:8) and that God has "prepared a table before you" (Psalm 23:5). It does not matter what happened to you or who dropped you; being crippled does not have to be the end of your story. The King of Kings is calling you by name, and he wants to take you out of your hurt place and bring you to a healed place. He wants to show you kindness, restore you, and he wants you to eat at his table. This table is a table of joy, peace, healing, blessings, victory, and favor. Therefore, it is imperative that you experience inner healing and deliverance. Not just so you can be healed, but so that you can experience the life that Jesus died for you to have.

> *"I am come that they might have life, and that they might have it more abundantly." (John 10:10)*

SIX EFFECTS OF TRAUMA

Trauma is the result of an event. It is the response to a distressing event that overwhelms your ability to cope appropriately. Trauma impacts you in various areas. The diagram below shows the six areas that are impacted by trauma.

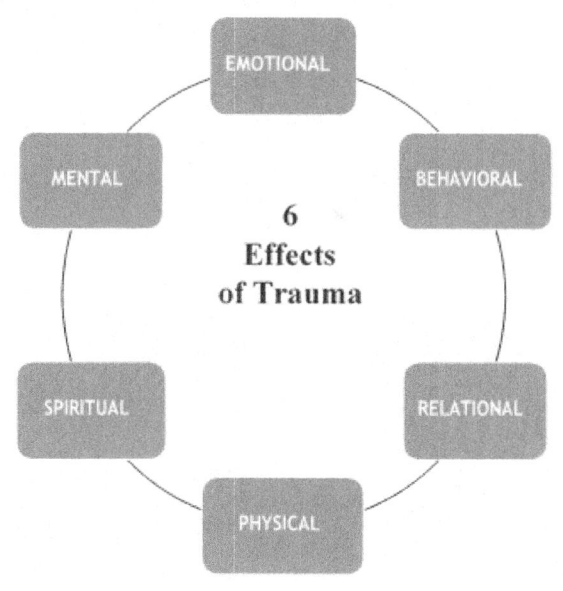

6 Effects of Trauma

- EMOTIONAL
- BEHAVIORAL
- RELATIONAL
- PHYSICAL
- SPIRITUAL
- MENTAL

"

The King of Kings is calling you by name, and he wants to take you out of your hurt place and bring you to a healed place. He wants to show you kindness, restore you, and he wants you to eat at his table.

"

Emotional Effects of Trauma

Emotions are neither good nor bad; they are what makes us human. Just like happiness is a part of being human, sadness, fear, and anger are a part of being human. The Bible states there is:

> *"A time to weep, and a time to laugh; a time to mourn, and a time to dance;" (Ecclesiastes 3:4)*

Our positive and negative emotional experiences are necessary to keep us balanced as humans and are necessary for survival. I recall my little brother and I were kids playing on a field. We noticed two big dogs that jumped a fence and were headed straight towards us. The fear we felt was necessary energy to assist us with running, and boy, did we run! We should not hide or suppress our emotions but learn to manage them and express them in healthy, nondestructive ways.

Before trauma, your emotional functioning is normal. When you experience trauma, your emotions are usually thrown off balance. You either become hyper-emotional or hypo. Instead of your emotional responses being a balance of 5, which is normal, you operate at the extremes of either 1 or a 10, or you become bipolar and jump from 1 to 10 and from 10 to 1. Some people lose emotional control because the suppressed pain causes an intense emotional trigger.

There was a client who was late for his session with me. He shared with me that while driving to my office, being only blocks away, someone cut him off and then beeped their horn at him. He said he became so angry that he grabbed a hammer, jumped out of his car, and headed towards the vehicle. Even though he called himself a Christian, his intention was not to pray for the man. Thank God the man quickly drove off when he recognized how manic my client was. I asked him if he was usually explosive. He explained to me that this occurrence was not an isolated incident, but he has a pattern of being overly aggressive and violent at times.

Usually, the way people act in one incident is a pattern of behavior. I knew the real issue was not that he was cut off but that he had a buildup of unresolved issues that was showing up as anger.

Some people's trauma causes them to become a time bomb ready to explode or implode. An indicator of open wounds from your past is that your emotional response does not match your current circumstance. Usually, the present issue is not the real issue; it exposes that there is a much deeper problem. For example, someone can lose their job and contemplate suicide. The root issue connected to the suicidal ideations is not that they lost their job. Many people lose their jobs but do not think about killing themselves. People who commit suicide do not really want to die; they want to escape the internal pain. Typically, the inner pain is intense because they have a buildup of trauma that overwhelms them. Not only is there a buildup, they lack the proper coping skills to deal with the pain. The present situation only triggers wounds from the past and causes what has already been in them to come to the surface and boil over.

As I began to assess my client, that almost assaulted a man with a hammer minutes before he came to see me, the truth behind his explosiveness was brought to the surface. He had a history of physical and sexual abuse that caused him to become an angry, volatile Christian. The lesson here is that your past chaos will cause you to create chaos in your present- day. When you do not address past pain, commonly, you become destructive to yourself or others. Therefore, healing is necessary so that you can live a productive life.

> *An indicator that there are open wounds from your past is that your emotional response does not match your current circumstance.*

There are two things that are an indicator that your emotional experience is abnormal. It is the longevity and the intensity. If you go to a therapist and tell them that you are feeling sad, they will ask you two questions: How intense is it on some sort of scale and how long does it last? If you say you feel sad occasionally and that it's a level 4, that's considered normal. However, people who suffer trauma develop abnormal emotional functioning. This means instead of a level 4 to 5, their emotional levels are at a 10 to 12 or 0 to 2 and occurs frequently or seasonally. Either they are hypersensitive or desensitized.

Hypersensitivity means your emotional response is over the top—you overreact. You become easily angered or easily offended. Desensitized is you have low to no emotional response. Here, this person diminishes any emotional response to a negative, adverse situation. Trauma can cause you to be hyperactive or inactive. In addition, it becomes difficult for you to regulate your emotions. Instead of you controlling your emotions, your emotions are controlling you. You are like a car that has no brakes. Once you get started, you cannot stop. You seem to be always sad, angry, anxious, etc. Also, you experience more negative emotions than positive because the negative emotions drown out positive ones.

I have noticed that as soon as a person gets free from their inner wounds, they can get filled with God's love, joy, and peace. God cannot fill you with these things if you already have other things like anger, bitterness, hurt, doubt, anxiety, and unforgiveness dominating your inner space. Experiencing inner healing typically enhances your relationship with God because you are open to receive his love, peace, and joy.

Behavioral Effects of Trauma

In the Bible, King David's son, Amnon raped his half-sister, Tamar. Not only was this traumatic for Tamar, but it was devastating to her brother Absalom. What made it even worse is that his father, King David, did what a lot of families do when made aware of sexual abuse within the home—he never addressed it. From that point forward, the Bible goes through narrative after narrative of Absalom's rebellious, defiant, and destructive behavior:

> 2 Samuel 13:28—Absalom kills his brother Amnon.
>
> 2 Samuel 14:30—Absalom sets Joab's field on fire.
>
> 2 Samuel 15:12—He conspires to kill his father, King David, and David flees for his life.
>
> 2 Samuel 16:22—He has sex with his father's concubines on the house top for Israel to see.

It is easy for us to label Absalom as having some sort of mental disorder or call him a thug. However, it is important to understand that Absalom was acting out of pain. His hostile behavior was connected to trauma. Unfortunately, the issue was never addressed and in 2 Samuel chapter 18, Absalom's behavior led to his demise—he was murdered. I believe if Absalom's pain was attended to, he could have been healed and became a productive person. Instead of focusing on what he was doing, the focus should have been on *why* he was doing it. King David could have taken a day off to lead his family to healing. Instead, King David pretended as if nothing happened and kept running his kingdom and writing psalms.

Absalom's internal conflict began to cause external damage and he had no one to turn to for support. Instead of listening to him, he was labeled. He saw his father counseling everyone else and helping them with their issues but not addressing his children's challenges. I believe many of the violence we see in our families and communities is connected to unhealed family trauma. Typically, you can trace a child's issue with something that is connected to the parent. If the home is where the hurt is happening, then where does the healing happen? I believe the church should be a safe place where people can come to get the healing they need. Not only will this contribute to us having healthy churches, but also healthy families and communities.

In summation, below are some of the behavioral effects of trauma:

- **Self-sabotaging:** Patterns of behavior and decisions that hinder you from accomplishing your goals or puts you in unwanted predicaments.
- **Low Self-control:** The inability to restrain oneself from actions that are outside of one's integrity or moral guidelines.
- **Impulsive:** Reacting from urges without properly thinking things through.
- **Compulsive:** Repeated behaviors that are outside of one's desire.
- **Unhealthy Coping Mechanisms or Self-medicating:** Any method used to deal with pain that is not beneficial to self. For example: trying to regulate oneself by indulging in unbiblical sex, shopping sprees, overeating, overworking, drugs, etc.
- **Explosive or Acting Out:** Outbursts of anger that are out of

control, damaging, and usually make you feel guilty afterward.

- **Perfectionism:** Having unrealistic expectations of oneself and others to do everything right and not giving the grace to make mistakes.
- **Disorganized:** Confused or cluttered thoughts which causes a lack of ability to have a structured life.
- **Inconsistent:** Starting tasks but not finishing them. Not seeing things through to the end. A pattern of giving up on one's commitment.
- **Controlling:** Trying to dominate a person or thing due to insecurity, fears, or doubts about yourself.
- **Passive:** The lack of assertiveness and speaking up for yourself and being timid and allowing people to take advantage of you.
- **Aggressive:** A pattern of hostile behavior that can cause harm to self or others. This includes verbal abuse.

Relational Effects of Trauma

You must heal from your past so that you can have healthy relationships. Every intimate relationship has a honeymoon stage. This is the stage where you cannot stay away from each other, you spend long nights on the phone, and every time you see them butterflies flutter in your stomach. Although this stage is important to bring you together, it will not keep you together. What will keep you together is that both of you have the capacity and compatibility to meet each other's needs.

If a person is not healed, not only will they not meet your needs, but they will hurt you when they should be helping you. One of the main questions you should ask someone before getting into an intimate relationship with them is, "Are you healed yet?" This would be a good conversation piece during a date. I do not recommend getting into a committed relationship until you understand a person's psychosocial history. You want to know their family structure and what it was like to grow up in their household. You want to understand what their father and mother were like or if they were in their life at all. You want to know the trauma they have experienced in their families and past relationships. You may think this is extreme, but you should act with extreme caution when you're considering spending your life with someone. The closest person to you can do you the most damage if they are not whole. The can cause you the most joy or the most pain.

Past relationships usually determine how you will function in your current relationship. There are specific characteristics and behavioral patterns that are transferred through growing up in your household. There is a phenomenon called *reenactment patterns* where you repeat a traumatic event or its circumstance over and over. One example is if an individual is raised in an abusive home and marries someone abusive just like their mother or father, or you grow up to be that abusive parent or spouse. It is imperative that you have these tough conversations with your significant other before you say, "I do." You must find out if they are healed from their trauma. If not, they will most likely sabotage the relationship and it will eventually deteriorate or both parties stay together but will be miserable.

I have had hundreds of counseling sessions where the husband or wife is having difficulty with their marriage because their spouse's unaddressed, unhealed issues are showing up in the marriage. In addition to the issues, the person lacks conflict resolution skills because they are emotionally unstable. Instead of problem-solving, they resort to verbal attacks and yelling, or they will avoid, shut down, and not speak about an issue that needs to be discussed. Healthy people know how to handle conflict in a healthy manner. Broken people have a dysfunctional way of handling problems in relationships.

ARE YOU THE FIXER

Another error that I see in relationships is when a person believes they can fix their significant other. During the dating stage, a person will act a certain way that reveals something is wrong. Instead of you taking this as a warning sign and a red flag that they're probably not the one, you believe you can fix them. The chances that you will fix them are very small, especially with a person that does not want to be fixed. Usually, you are not the first person that has had this problem with this person, and if they have not addressed it in their past relationships, they are probably not going to address it with you. Quite frankly some people need deliverance and you're so blinded by their beauty that you don't know you're dating a demon.

A person must be willing to get the help they need. If you try to fix someone who is not sincerely willing to get the help they need, you will enable them. Enablers do not make the situation better; they make it worse. An enabler is a person who encourages negative or self-destructive behavior in another while thinking they're helping. But the person will manipulate your love and compassion and use you as a crutch. Instead of being challenged to change, they will become comfortable because of how you care for them. Some people need to experience a crisis to change, and some need to lose to gain.

To change, the prodigal son needed to hit rock bottom and have nobody to turn to. Notice when he told his father that he was leaving, his father did not try to stop him or coddle him. His father let him go so that he could hit rock bottom and learn the lesson.

> *"To illustrate the point further, Jesus told them this story: "A man had two sons. The younger son told his father, 'I want my share of your estate now before you die.' So, his father agreed to divide his wealth between his sons. "A few days later this younger son packed all his belongings and moved to a distant land, and there he wasted all his money in wild living. About the time his money ran out, a great famine swept over the land, and he began to starve. He persuaded a local farmer to hire him, and the man sent him into his fields to feed the pigs. The young man became so hungry that even the pods he was feeding the pigs looked good to him. But no one gave him anything. "When he finally came to his senses, he said to himself, 'At home even the hired servants have food enough to spare, and here I am dying of hunger! I will go home to my father and say, "Father, I have sinned against both heaven and you, and I am no longer worthy of being called your son. Please take me on as a hired servant." (Luke 15: 11-17)*

The consequences of the prodigal son's actions caused him to come to his senses. His father knew that he couldn't fix his son; his son had to come to the place where he wanted to change. The father loved him enough to release him. The prodigal son left stubborn, rebellious, and immature but returned repentant, humble, and transformed. Sometimes, you may believe that you are helping someone when you're hurting them. Enablers help negate the consequences brought on by someone else's behavior. They are always willing to give one more chance, and then another and another. But you must love people enough to learn how to say no and let them go. You may feel afraid that something terrible will happen, but you are not responsible for what happens to them. What happens to them is a result of the decisions they

The Impact of Trauma

make. Allowing them to experience the consequences of their actions by not enabling them will give them a chance to change. This is what happened in the story of the prodigal son.

> *You must love people enough to learn how to say no and let them go.*

There was a young man who was kicked out of college. He came home expecting his parents to let him move back into their home. His father met him at the door and told him he could not come home. As a result, he became homeless and lived and slept in his car for months. This resulted in him learning his lesson, changing his attitude, and getting serious about his life, and today he is a millionaire. What would have happened if his father would have let him back in his house? He would have enabled him, and the young man would quite possibly never learned his lesson.

I had a lady come to me because she was newly married, and her husband, who was twice her size, physically attacked her. He slammed her so hard on the ground that she was having back problems. She asked me what she should do, and I told her to call the police. She stated that she loved him and did not want to call the police. I told her the best thing that she could do for him and herself is call the police. I told her if he was arrested and went to jail, he would think twice about harming her again. I want to reiterate that some people will not change unless they experience the consequences for their actions.

It is nobody's responsibility to fix you but yours. People can support you during your healing process, but you must be willing to get the help you need and do the work to become whole. You may need professional help and there is really nothing those close to you can do for you. The best thing someone can do for you is point you in the direction of a therapist, substance abuse program, or other resources that provide support for the issue you are dealing with.

You cannot have healthy relationships if you are broken. Your pain will spread to those closest to you. That thing that happened to you that you thought you buried will eventually resurrect. That pain inside of you will be like poison. It will show up in various ways and contaminate people you care about. Some entire families have been adversely affected because a father or a mother didn't get the healing they needed. Your motivation to heal should not just be about you but those closest to you. If you don't want to do it for yourself, do it for them.

In summation, here are some of the relationship impacts of trauma:

- **Isolating:** Avoids being around people. Pulls away from those they should be pulling close to.
- **Numbing:** Not emotionally present in a relationship. Lack of affection and emotional expression.
- **Codependent:** Overly attached and dependent on another person for emotional balance and security.
- **Abusive:** Verbally, physically, emotionally, or mentally violent towards a person.
- **Difficulty Forgiving:** Holds on to offense. Finds it difficult to forgive and move on.
- **Controlling:** Dominating and demanding. Does not allow a

person's individuality and freedom.

- **Issues With Intimacy:** Has a low sex drive and lack of affection or is hypersexual and unfaithful to a spouse. Struggles with infidelity or pornography.

- **Reenactment Patterns:** Continues the traumatic cycle by allowing the same type of treatment as an adult. Two examples are a person who was abused as a child gets involved in abusive relationships as an adult or a person who is molested as a child gets involved in ungodly sexual acts and perversion as an adult. My experience with counseling Christian men who struggled with homosexuality is that they were usually molested by males as a child or the victim of incest from a male family member.

- **Role Reversal:** You begin to treat people how you were treated. The victim becomes the victimizer. An example is a person who was abused by their caretaker and grows up to become the abuser as an adult.

- **Low Conflict Resolution Skills:** Resorts to arguing, yelling, and verbal attacks instead of working towards a solution in a civil manner.

- **Passive:** Does not speak up for themselves, people pleaser, or find it difficult to say no.

- **Aggressive:** Very angry and hostile towards people.

- **Projections:** A coping mechanism in which a person attributes how they feel about themselves onto others. For example, a person who is self-conscious about their weight might feel like everyone views them as "fat."

Physical Effects of Trauma

I had a client in his early thirties who came to see me for inner healing and deliverance sessions due to problems he was having in his body. He had been to the doctor because he was showing symptoms of a heart attack. After they conducted tests, they could not find anything physically wrong. Finally, they told him that it was psychosomatic, and if he did not address his mental and emotional stress, he would have a heart attack and die.

During the session, I discovered that he had a lot of unresolved grief from people close to him who had died. The result of him not grieving and holding in all his emotions was beginning to affect his heart. This was caused by him being taught that it was weak for a man to cry. This belief system backfired, and because of not crying, his heart was now weak. To heal physically, he needed to release his repressed grief through grieving. I had him picture the people he had lost, get in touch with the pain, and allow himself to cry. This was very therapeutic for him, and he began to improve.

I have had several sessions where people received inner healing and deliverance, *and* their physical body was healed! There was a pastor's wife that was in a group session. She almost did not make it to the session because her entire body was in excruciating pain. Instead of going to the hospital, she decided to come to the group session. As I walked them through receiving inner healing through forgiveness, she began to weep, and then demons began coming out of her. Suddenly, she testified that while that was happening, she felt the presence of God throughout her body. It started at her feet and began flowing up through her entire body. After that phenomenon was over, all the pain left her body, and she was healed.

Studies have proved that 80% of illness is connected to some mental or emotional distress or stress. Pent-up emotional trauma not only adversely affects your mind and emotions, but it also has a direct impact on you physically. You can become ill and even die from unaddressed trauma.

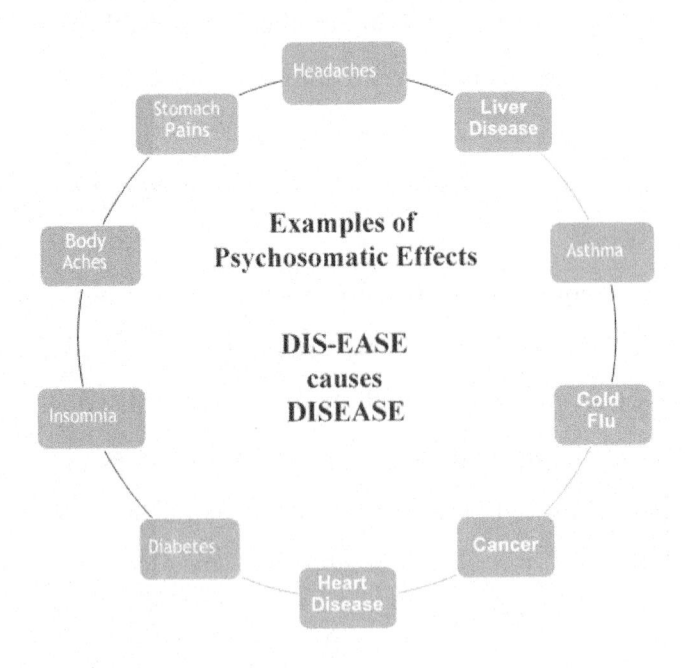

Examples of Psychosomatic Effects

DIS-EASE causes DISEASE

- Headaches
- Liver Disease
- Asthma
- Cold Flu
- Cancer
- Heart Disease
- Diabetes
- Insomnia
- Body Aches
- Stomach Pains

Removing Pain from Your Body

Pain can become trapped in your body if not properly processed. Bioenergetic therapy theory believes that pain can be held in various parts of the body. As a result, it can manifest itself physically through sickness, aches, tension, headaches, sleep disturbance, and other manifestations. This form of therapy works with the body and mind to help people resolve their emotional problem. For healing to occur, you must locate that part of the body where the pain is and release that pain through expression and movement.

I have experienced this myself. I was at a "GUTS" bioenergetic facilitation training, and while we were in a circle, they asked if anyone wanted to do some "work." Since my best way of learning and testing a therapeutic model is to experience it myself, I quickly stepped into the middle of the circle. I knew that I was carrying unaddressed pain from something that happened to me when I was twelve.

As I stood in the circle, two counselors stood in front of me to facilitate my healing process. I closed my eyes, pictured myself as that twelve-year-old boy, and they had me tell my story of what happened that hurt me. Suddenly, I could feel the repressed subconscious pain that I was carrying since I was twelve began to manifest in a specific part of my body. As I touched the area where the pain was located, I felt my body wanting to cry.

Crying is one way that the body releases pain. Failing to cry causes pain to become stuck in your body. As I welcomed the feeling to cry, I allowed myself to weep as hard and as loud as I needed to. Suddenly, just by allowing myself to cry, I experienced catharsis and felt the pain leave my body.

One time, I was doing trauma training and walking participants through a group inner healing and deliverance session. I facilitated them into picturing the people who hurt them and releasing the pain that came up for them. I provided them with a safe, sacred space to do whatever they needed to express the pain. Some people yelled, some people said words like, "I hate you!," and some cried. Afterward, they stated how they felt relieved and free because they addressed things they had been holding in for years.

LET IT OUT

Your emotions are meant to be expressed not suppressed. When your body is experiencing an emotion, it organically wants to let that emotion out. There's always a motion connected to an emotion. If you feel happy on the inside, your body naturally wants to laugh. If you feel fear, your body naturally wants to scream, run, or hide. If you are angry, your body naturally wants to do something aggressive to release that anger. In my practice, I have found it very therapeutic and healing to provide a person space to allow themselves to release what they have been carrying. I ask questions like, "If that feeling could talk or do something, what would it be?" "If that anger could do something, what would it be? If that sadness had a sound, what would it sound like?"

You don't need a therapist to release emotional triggers. Kind David did it through playing an instrument and writing psalms. From my therapeutic lens, the book of Psalms was not just about King David praising God, but there were many passages where he was expressing and releasing his pain, anger, and frustration. There is a pattern in many of King David's writings when he would go from a complaint to praise. Even though there is an erroneous saying that men don't cry, the word cry is mentioned twenty-nine times in the book of Psalms. Here's one example of David expressing his concerns and calling out to God for help through a song.

> *"LORD, how are they increased that trouble me! Many are they that rise up against me. Many there be which say of my soul, There is no help for him in God. Selah. But thou, O LORD, art a shield for me; My glory, and the lifter up of mine head. I cried unto the LORD with my voice, And he heard me out of his holy hill. Selah." (Psalms 3:1-4)*

Job expressed his grief when he found out that his children were killed.

> *"While he was still speaking, another messenger arrived with this news: "Your sons and daughters were feasting in their oldest brother's home. Suddenly, a powerful wind swept in from the wilderness and hit the house on all sides. The house collapsed, and all your children are dead.*

I am the only one who escaped to tell you." Job stood up and tore his robe in grief. Then he shaved his head and fell to the ground to worship." (Job 1:18-20 NLT)

Jesus let out his sadness in the Garden of Gethsemane through expressing his feeling to his disciples and going before Father God in prayer.

"And he took with him Peter and the two sons of Zebedee, and began to be sorrowful and very heavy. Then saith he unto them, My soul is exceeding sorrowful, even unto death: tarry ye here, and watch with me. And he went a little further, and fell on his face, and prayed, saying, O my Father, if it be possible, let this cup pass from me: nevertheless not as I will, but as thou wilt." (Matthew 26:37-39)

Here are some ways you can release negative emotions:

- Speak to someone about how you feel.
- Grab a pillow and give that feeling a sound. Release that energy into the pillow.
- Pray to God and tell him about your feelings.
- Write about your feelings or have a "feelings journal."
- Take deep breaths and breathe into the emotions.
- Allow yourself space to cry.
- Scream as loud and as much as you need to until you feel a release.
- Locate on your body where the emotion is and move that area of your body as you imagine shaking it off.
- Punch something – not somebody – until you feel better.

Negative emotions typically only last up to thirty minutes if appropriately processed. If not properly released, what should be temporary will become permanent, and demonic spirts can enter. What you bury you will carry. When you're feeling that hurt, grief, anger, or anxiety, there are ways you can release it to get it out. You can write it out, talk it out with someone you trust, or act it out. All you need to do is be in a safe space, maybe by yourself, and allow yourself to scream, cry, or hit something and let that negative energy out. If you're not harming yourself or anyone around you, it's good to let those emotions out.

Once you release it, then you can decide what to do with it. Do you want to hold on to it or let it go? Do you want to worry about it or give it to God? Do you want to stay mad and upset, or do you want to forgive so you can move forward?

Spiritual Effects of Trauma

Ephesians 5:18-19 tells us to be angry but do not sin, and do not allow the sun to go down while we are still angry. This scripture further explains what happens when you hold on to anger. Verse 19 states that if you hold on to anger you are giving a place or residence for a demon spirit to enter. We can conclude from these passages that whatever you hold on to, the spirit of that thing can enter you. An example is if you hold on to depression, a spirit of depression will enter. If you hold on to fear, then a spirit of fear will enter. This is not to say that as Christians we do not experience sadness, hurt, anger, or fear. These are normal human emotions, but to constantly be in this type of emotional state is abnormal, unhealthy, toxic, and opens doors for demons to enter. As Christians, it is imperative for us to monitor our emotional state. Things will get on us, but it does not have to get in us.

In 2 Samuel chapter 12, King David's wife was pregnant and the child in her womb was sick unto death. David was so distraught and in so much pain and grief that he refused to eat, shave, or change his clothes. This was a traumatic moment for David. Once he found out his child died, the Bible says David got up, worshipped God, and then ate. I believe David did this because he realized that he could not stay stuck in that emotional state. He had a kingdom to run, a wife to attend to, people to lead, and a God to serve. The key to David not getting stuck in grief and the pain of his son's death was that he worshipped God. I believe praise and worship is the key to Christians staying free. The Bible is full of scriptures that instructs Christians to live a life of worship, praise, and joy, because it keeps you free from allowing contrary toxic emotions to linger.

> *"Rejoice in the Lord always: and again, I say, Rejoice." (Philippians 4:4)*

> *"Rejoice evermore. Pray without ceasing. In everything give thanks: for this is the will of God in Christ Jesus concerning you." (1 Thessalonians 5:16-18)*

> *"I will bless the Lord at all times: his praise shall continually be in my mouth." (Psalm 34:1)*

Demons Connected to Trauma

It is important to understand that what is worse than the trauma itself is not being healed from the trauma. You carry the mental and emotional damage from past trauma into your present life, and you will carry demons that entered because of that trauma into your present-

The Impact of Trauma

day. The following is a list of demon spirits I have encountered from facilitating deliverance with people who have experienced trauma.

Encountered Demon Spirits	
Infirmity	Depression
Confusion	Low Self-Esteem
Suicide	Lunatic
Torment	Perversion
Jezebel	Rebellion
Rage	Murder
Hate	Unforgiveness
Bitterness	Shame
Envy	Fear

To properly cast these demons out, so that you can get free and stay free, the trauma must be healed before deliverance. Dealing with the demon before addressing the trauma not only causes deliverance to be difficult, but the evil spirits will just come back because you are not addressing the root cause of why the demons are there. Remember, demons feed off hurt and pain. When you are healed, the demon has nothing to feed on and becomes weak. After your healing, your deliverance is imminent.

Mental Effects of Trauma

Trauma can have a serious impact on the mind. There are three mental effects of trauma:

- Wounded Messages
- Wounded Identity
- Wounded Memory

Wounded Messages	Wounded Identity	Wounded Memory
The pain is ingrained in the messages	Your identity is not how people see you; it's how you see yourself	Pain connected to the memory of what happened
Cognitive distortions	Negative self-perception	
Lies	Low self-esteem	
	Self-hate	
	Pretending Being somebody you're not because you do not like who you are, and you don't know who you are	

For deep-level freedom to take place, each of these areas must be healed.

Wounded Messages

There is always a message connected to a wound. Some people are not aware of these messages because they could be subconscious messages or messages they have normalized. These painful messages are what feeds the emotional wounds.

The Impact of Trauma

According to Cognitive Behavioral Therapy Theory, your belief system drives your emotions, and your emotions drive your behavior. If you want to change how you act, you must change how you feel; and if you are going to change how you feel, you must change how you think. Romans 12:2 states, "Be ye transformed by the renewing of your mind…" According to this text, transformation happens, not by changing your behavior or feelings, but by changing what you are thinking. If you change your behavior without changing the way you think, you will only experience fleeting change, not true transformation.

To heal depression, you do not deal with the behavior. You must identify the feeling that is driving the behavior. Beyond that, you must identify the messages that are feeding the depressed emotions. You may be aware of the emotions but are you aware of the messages connected to the emotions? Usually, these messages are contracted at the point of the trauma and are carried throughout your life.

I had a client whose parents never paid attention to her and left her with a babysitter all the time. Her parents were verbally abusive and would say harsh things to her. As a result, she felt that something was wrong with her, and she was not lovable. These messages were birthed through the traumatic experience and carried into her adult life. A part of her healing was identifying and renouncing these messages.

One method you can do to identify wounded messages you are carrying is to name the feelings connected to the trauma. Now if those feelings could talk, what would they say about you? I use this method quite often in my practice. Once I trace the wound, I have the client get in touch with their hurt, name the feelings, and give it a voice. Now that they have identified it, they must go through the therapeutic process of changing it.

> If you change your behavior without changing the way you think, you will only experience fleeting change, not true transformation.

Wounded Identity

Your identity is not how people see you, it is how you see yourself. Trauma damages your identity. You develop a distorted view of yourself. As a result of traumatic events, you can develop a negative self-perception. This causes low-self- esteem, insecurity, negative self-talk, and even self-hate. This is because you have a hard time separating what happened to you from who you are. You are confusing what you have been through with who you are. People who suffer sexual abuse have a damaged sense of self. What happened to them was shameful, perverted, and disgusting, so they see themselves as that. They have difficulty separating what happened to them from who they are. What the individual did to them becomes integrated into their self-perception.

A part of the healing process is getting your identity restored so that you can have a healthy sense of self. It would help if you separated what happened to you from who you are. You are not what happened to you; you have just been negatively impacted by it. You must learn how to see yourself through the eyes of Father God. God does not look at you and see your mess or your misery; he sees you as his son or daughter.

> *"How precious also are thy thoughts unto me, O God! how great is the sum of them! If I should count them, they are more in number than the sand: when I awake, I am still with thee." (Psalm 139:17-18)*

Healing from rejection has nothing to do with your being accepted by people and has everything to do with you accepting yourself.

When you accept that God loves you for who you are, you can learn to accept and love yourself for who you are. When this happens, you are not concerned about whether people accept you or not. When you know that God validates you and you learn to validate yourself, you do not seek validation from others. Rejection has nothing to do with whether people accept you or not; it is rooted in the fact that you do not accept yourself. When you love and accept yourself, it does not matter who rejects you because you know your value. You will realize that it is their loss, not yours, and that you are not the problem; they are.

How you see yourself impacts how you perceive other people see you. Sometimes what you think people see is not what they really see. You have a distorted view of how people see you and do not realize it. Your perception is not necessarily reality, but your perception is *your* reality. When you have a negative view of yourself, you can project how you see yourself onto others. You can be thinking *they don't like me*, and it is not that they do not like you; you do not like yourself. Since you do not like yourself, you are strategically and sometimes subconsciously sabotaging your relationship with others.

Wounded Memory

I had a client who had several traumatic events from age five up until thirty-five. I walked her through each adverse incident she experienced. Interestingly, she was miraculously and powerfully healed and delivered from one event, but when I walked her through another event, it had its own set of wounds and demons. Our memory is like a storage facility with various units or compartments. We can compartmentalize by separating the different parts or events of our lives. Within those units are its own set of traumatic memories, pain, and demons. Therefore, it is important to get healing around every traumatic event that you have ever experienced. If you fail to address each area, you can receive partial healing and deliverance in one area but still be bound and wounded in another.

On numerous occasions, I have heard people say that they wanted God to erase their bad memories because of a traumatic experience. There are certain things that our mind will not forget. People may think they have forgotten, but do not realize that the memory is still alive in the subconscious. The dilemma is not the memory, it is the pain that is connected to the memory. As soon as the memory is healed, there is no pain, and the memory can be used for the glory of God.

You do not want your memory to be erased because your story has value. People need to hear your story. Your story can set someone else free that is going through the same thing that you have been through. Your ministry may be connected to your story. Some people use their traumatic memory to write books, counsel others, in motivational speaking, etc. Your memory can be a testimony to how God has brought you out. God does not want you to forget it because he wants you to use it to help someone else and not forget what he brought you out of.

Chapter 8

Why It's Not God's Fault

In my sessions, I have seen people blame God for unfortunate events, but I must tell you that he has nothing to do with it. As a pastor in the inner city, I was the eulogist for several young individuals in their twenties and even teens who were gunned down because of violence or their involvement in criminal activity. At one funeral, I was disturbed because a preacher stood up, approached the pulpit, and stated to the grieving family and those in attendance that God had a purpose behind the young person being gunned down. He continued by saying it was God's will, and they should accept God's plan. Sadly, to say, this was not God's purpose, plan, or will, but the result of the individual's poor choices. My brother was murdered at the age of twenty-two. It was painful, but I had to accept the decisions he made in life led to the events that caused him to lose his life. This was not God's fault or will.

When a person blames God, they block God from comforting or healing them because of offense they are carrying against God.

When a person over spiritualizes—placing a greater spiritual significance on something than they should—and do other things like blame the devil or God or say that God told them things that he did not tell them, they fail to take ownership for where they are in life or the decisions they have made. Consequently, they do not do what they need to do to change and heal because they believe nothing is their fault.

When a person blames God, they block God from comforting or healing them because of offense they are carrying against God. Truthfully, there are many things that happen on this earth that is not God's will or purpose. Here is a scripture that proves that.

> *"The Lord is not slack concerning his promise, as some men count slackness; but is longsuffering to us-ward, not willing that any should perish, but that all should come to repentance." (2 Peter 3:9)*

Although it is God's desire that no one should spend eternity in hell, people are going to hell because of their choices not to serve Jesus Christ. This is a testament to the fact that God has chosen to give mankind free will. As a result, God does not force his way into our lives or situations or force us to obey him. It must be voluntary. Jesus states that he cannot come into our lives unless he is invited. He said,

> *"Behold, I stand at the door, and knock: if any man hear my voice, and open the door, I will come in to him, and will sup with him, and he with me." (Revelation 3:20).*

Consider the fact that there is no sickness, no sadness, and no problems in heaven because God is the ruler. However, on earth, God has given man authority and with authority comes responsibility and consequences for actions outside of God's will.

I was coming home from church with my five-year-old daughter and my mother in the car. My daughter is very inquisitive and asks lots of questions. While driving home she blurted out, "Daddy, why did God create bees and mosquitoes to hurt us if he loves us?" I consider myself a Bible scholar and have answered many complex questions in my day, but this time I was puzzled. Thank God for Grandma! She said, "In the beginning it wasn't like this. God created all living creatures to live in harmony. After Adam and Eve sinned, sin entered the world which caused animals to harm each other and us." This is not just the case with bees and mosquitoes harming mankind; as a result of a history of mankind choosing to live life outside of God's will, it invites disorder, trauma, and demonic activity on all levels. There are all types of evil and demonic activity that enters families and affects innocent children all because of the ungodly choices of the parents and ancestors. It is not God's will, but it is our decisions that exclude God and are inclusive for demonic spirits.

I had a woman who blamed God for the man she was in a relationship with because she said that God told her that he was her husband. But God did not tell her that because the man was not saved, and the Bible clearly says, "Be not unequally yoked together with unbelievers…what fellowship has light with darkness" (2 Corinthians 6:14-15). God never tells us anything that goes against his word. This person was in error and used God to justify what her flesh wanted, and she was paying the consequences.

This is also an issue when people receive false prophecies. I have had sessions with a myriad of people who were awfully angry at God because of a prophecy they received that either did not happen or caused them to make poor decisions. Instead of realizing that the person who prophesied to them was in error, they blamed God for it not happening or materializing and then falling apart. It is important to understand what the Bible says about prophecy:

> "Beloved, believe not every spirit, but try the spirits whether they are of God: because many false prophets are gone out into the world." (1 John 4:1)

> "And if thou say in thine heart, How shall we know the word which the Lord hath not spoken? When a prophet speaketh in the name of

Why It's Not God's Fault

> the Lord, if the thing follow not, nor come to pass, that is the thing which the Lord hath not spoken, but the prophet hath spoken it presumptuously: thou shalt not be afraid of him." (Deuteronomy 18:21-22)

One of the reasons why people cannot heal is because they blame God. I have had countless clients that were upset with God. They erroneously accused him. "Why did he allow this to happen?" "Why didn't God stop it?" "Why didn't God protect me?" Let me be candid: stop blaming God for what people did to you. When you blame God, you block God from healing you. I want to take some time to explain why it is not God's fault. Even though God is all-powerful, he is limited by his word. His word says the following:

> "The heaven, even the heavens, are the Lord's: but the earth hath he given to the children of men." (Psalm 115:16)

When God gave man authority over the earth, he limited himself. This means that God does nothing on earth without working through man. God needs man's permission or submission to intervene and work on earth. If you look through the Bible, anything God did, he did through man. Any ungodliness or evil that happened, it happened because man forsook God, disobeyed God, and chose their own ways.

> "And God said, Let us make man in our image, after our likeness: and let them have dominion over the fish of the sea, and over the fowl of the air, and over the cattle, and over all the earth, and over every creeping thing that creepeth upon the earth." (Genesis 1:26)

According to God's divine structure, man has dominion or ruling authority over the earth. As long as Adam and Eve followed God's plan, there was peace and prosperity. When they disobeyed God, they invited sin into their heart and into their family. Cain killed his brother Abel because God accepted Abel's offering over Cain's (Genesis 4:8). This was a result of Adam and Eve's decision that opened the door for sin. It was not God's fault or his plan for Cain to kill his brother Abel. Situations like these have been happening since the fall of man, and it is not God's will. When King David committed adultery and slept with Bathsheba, he opened the door for a spirit of perversion and murder to enter his family (2 Samuel 11). The chain of events that happened were not God's fault or plan but due to David's bad decisions and poor parenting.

God's purpose for this world was peace and harmony, but when you look at world events, you see war, division, and chaos. This is a result of man's sin, indiscretion, and excluding God from his plans. Consider terrorism, sex trafficking, police brutality or racism; none of this is God's will or plan on this earth. When you contemplate what man calls "acts of nature" such as fires that destroy our forests, tsunamis that devastate communities, or the increase in tornadoes that obliterate homes and businesses, these are really acts of man. Due to man not properly caring for the earth that God has placed us in charge of, and instead polluting the earth, this has caused global warming. Global warming throws the earth's equilibrium off which causes these "acts of nature." Scientists have stated that if humanity does not take better care of the earth, eventually, there will not be an earth to live in.

Here is a more personal example. It is not logical for you to choose to eat unhealthily and blame God because you are sick. Then, as Christians, we have the religious nerve to pray over our unhealthy food and ask God to "bless it and make it a nourishment to our bodies." Your ailment is the consequence of your actions and had nothing to do with God. Just because you prayed over that fried chicken – soaked in oil, drenched in hot sauce, and mild sauce – does not mean God makes it healthy. Now, when our arteries are clogged or diabetes sets in, we question God and ask him why he allowed it to happen. He allowed it because he has given you free will and he cannot violate the systems and laws he has put in place. Instead of charging God for your ailment, you need to change your diet. There is such a thing called cause and effect. If you want a different outcome, you must be determined to make different decisions. Change doesn't happen by chance; it happens by you making the right choices.

I had a client who was raped, and she blamed God. In the middle of the session, the Holy Spirit revealed to me that God told her not to date him and she chose not to listen. When I inquired about this, she confirmed that God warned her not to date this person, but she disobeyed. What happened to her was not God's will nor God's fault but a result of her not listening to God. Even in families, things happen in the home, not because it is God's fault but because of poor parenting or parents not making God a priority in the home.

Some things happen because of poor decisions we make. Some things happen because of the actions or decisions of those we are connected to or are close to. And then some things happen because it is a part of being human. When it comes to death, we think it is a bad thing. Death is not good or bad; it is natural. We were never meant to live on this earth for eternity, and death is how we transition from the natural world into the spiritual world. Hebrews 9:27 says, *"And as it is appointed unto men once to die, but after this the judgment:"*

Even though death is a normal process, people are upset at God for taking their loved one. But there is also the possibility for people to die before their time. This is not due to God's will but decisions an individual makes or another person makes that impact those around them. I served as eulogist for a young man who robbed a convenience store and was shot and killed by the clerk. A minister came up to have words and he said something regarding the young man's death that angered me. He said, "We never will understand God's will, but his plan is perfect." As I sat there in my anger, I thought to myself that it was not God's will nor plan for this young man to get shot and killed. I also thought about how his family could blame and be angry at God because of an erroneous statement from that minister.

So, you may be wondering how I know when it is God. You know it is God because it is not connected to evil or sin. The Bible lets us know:

> *"Let no man say when he is tempted, I am tempted of God: for God cannot be tempted with evil, neither tempteth he any man." (James 1:13)*

God is a holy God, and he does not cause evil. Wickedness is a result of man allowing sin into the world. The evil that happens is due to the mistakes of man, not God. The good news is that even though evil things happen that are not God's will, God can use it to work it out for your good. He can turn your pain into purpose and use it for his glory. What the devil meant to destroy you, God will use to develop and deploy you.

> What the devil meant to destroy you, God will use to develop and deploy you.

Apostle Paul was placed in prison by man due to him preaching the Gospel. God used this dire situation to work for Paul's good. Much of the New Testament was written by the apostle Paul while he was in prison. Similarly, Joseph was betrayed by his brothers (due to him bragging about his dreams), thrown in a pit, and ended up in prison. God used this adverse experience to prepare Joseph to be ruler in the palace, and it worked out for his good. Look at what Joseph said to his brothers who betrayed him because of jealousy:

> *"But as for you, ye thought evil against me; but God meant it unto good, to bring to pass, as it is this day, to save much people alive." (Genesis 50:20)*

Once Joseph was delivered from what his brothers did to him, he could walk in his purpose. God desires to heal you from the pain of your past so that you can walk in your purpose.

Chapter 9

Why the Devil is Not The Problem

Deliverance alone does not heal trauma because demons are not the cause of the trauma but can enter in because of a traumatic experience. For the sake of privacy, I have a young man named John come see me because of issues he was having as an adult which was a result of him being molested by his uncle when he was six years old. Trying to numb the pain independently, John became an alcoholic and struggled with hiring male prostitutes. I forgot to mention that John was a ministry leader at his church. John's struggle was not a result of demons but suppressed, unaddressed hurt from being molested. Casting demons out of John would undoubtedly make him feel better but would not bring healing and total freedom from the root cause of John's issue, which was trauma.

You need to understand that demons do not cause the issues, but they exacerbate them. Let us say you are dealing with anger, and on a scale of 1-10, your level of anger is at an 8. If a spirit of anger enters, it will take it from an 8 to a level 16. After the spirit is cast out, your level of anger would automatically go back down to an 8, but you would still need to deal with the wounds or issues connected to the anger.

This is precisely what I did with John. As he sat across from me and expressed his symptoms (alcoholism, male prostitution, and intense shame), I could trace it back to what caused John to live such a lifestyle—the unaddressed trauma from being molested as a child. As an adult, he worked in ministry to mask his pain. Eventually, the mask came off and John fell into sexual sin with another male in the church. Afterward, he sought support from his church but was ridiculed. This caused him to leave the church and go deeper into a sinful lifestyle. He then medicated himself from the hurt, pain, and shame by drinking alcohol daily. John sat across from me and expressed that he felt that God did not love him anymore and that God had forsaken him. The shame and abandonment were immense because of the rejection John felt from his church, which he attributed to how God felt about him.

I walked John through rededicating his life to Christ, and he immediately began to weep. He stated that he could feel Jesus's acceptance and affections towards him. He said that he could feel Jesus pour into him "peace, confidence, and integrity." I walked John through healing from the wound of being molested and rejected by the church using *God Therapy*. After the inner healing process was complete, I performed deliverance on John. With minimal effort, I said a short prayer and the demons immediately manifested and began to scream in torment. As the demons manifested, you could hear various voices coming out of John. It was like a demonic harmony of screeches. Within minutes, John was totally free and filled with the Holy Spirit. He began speaking in tongues and worshipping Jesus for his freedom.

Notice, before I dealt with the demon, I dealt with the wounds from his childhood which were the root cause. As soon as the wounds were healed and John forgave who he needed to forgive, the deliverance was easy, because the demon was not the cause of the issue but connected to the issue. I want to reiterate that the demon is not the problem, the demon is the result of the problem.

I can recall as a child, there was an infestation of roaches in our home. They were all in the kitchen cabinets, drawers, and crawling all around the floor. It was so bad that one day I was pouring cereal, and roaches came out of the cereal box. My question for you is this: Were the roaches the problem or the result of the problem? The problem was not the roaches, it was that my parents assigned my brothers, my sister, and me to clean the kitchen, and as teenagers usually do, we did a poor job at it. We barely swept the floor, did not clean the countertops off properly, and rushed through doing the dishes. I was guilty on multiple occasions of leaving food particles on the dishes after I washed them. It did not matter how many roaches we killed or how much roach spray we sprayed. The roaches kept coming back because we never addressed the root issue. They also began to spread to other parts of our home: the family room, bedrooms, and bathroom. You name it—they were there. Finally, my mom had us thoroughly clean out the entire kitchen. Then she hired someone to clean the kitchen more fervently. When this was complete, we addressed the roach issue and they never returned.

As previously stated, demons are like roaches: to survive, they need to be fed. A spirit of depression needs to feed off sadness, so they look for someone who is depressed. When a Christian believer gives in to the sadness and is not submitting to the scriptures that says, "Rejoice in the Lord always" (Philippians 4:4 KJV) or "Serve the Lord with gladness" (Psalm 100:2), then the demon can gain access and maintain because it's feeding. If a Christian is constantly depressed that means they are serving God with sadness, not gladness. Even if you resist the devil, it will not leave unless you are also submitted to God's word. According to the book of James, you must "Submit yourselves therefore to God" then "resist the devil and he will flee." (James 4:7). If I cast the devil out of you, but don't address the messages, wounds, or sin that it is feeding from, it will only come back. The roaches in my parents' home never returned, not because of the Raid, but because my parents made sure we cleaned the kitchen properly.

For you to be totally delivered from demons and stay free, you must be cleaned of sin, unforgiveness, wounds, and other things that demons feed off. Deliverance was never meant to be a revolving door. However, if you do not deal with the root, deliverance will seem difficult and unsustainable. Unfortunately, most deliverance ministers focus on the demon but do not address the demon's cause, and therefore, demon spirits keep gaining access.

For you to be totally delivered from demons and stay free, you must be cleaned of sin, unforgiveness, wounds, and other things that demons feed off.

Chapter 10

How Christians Become Demonized

I have found that there are four categories that Christians fall into that causes them to become demonized. They are either transferred over, they are not following God's word, they have partnered with a negative belief system, or are spiritually weak.

TRANSFERRED OVER

The experiences that happened to people or situations people became involved in before they gave their life to Jesus Christ open the door for demons to enter them. Although they accept the Lord as their Savior, those spirits are still there. A member of my church loved God and had a very humble, kind spirit but was a former gang member. To my surprise, when I performed deliverance on him, there were at least thirty demons from the things he did while in the gang that manifested and had to be cast out.

Demon spirits can also be transferred over through generational sins. Activities that your parents or ancestors were involved in open doors for demonic spirits. When they gain access, they have the legal right to transfer through the blood line. After a person gives their life to Christ, they must go through deliverance specifically to deal with generational sins and curses.

Finally, demonic spirits can be transferred over through trauma. To my surprise, about 90 percent of clients that came to see me for healing were molested. This included men and women. While walking them through deliverance, demons of perversion, low self-esteem, anger, hate, control, the spirit of Jezebel, and murder would manifest. It is not just molestation; demonic spirits can transfer over through any traumatic experience you have had throughout your life. Those demonic spirits do not automatically leave because you're a Christian. The trauma must be healed, and those demons need to be cast out.

NOT FOLLOWING GOD'S WORD

To live a healthy Christian life, the Bible instructs us that we should live by "every word that proceeds out of the mouth of God" (Matthew 4:4). Disobedience opens the door for demons. In 1 Samuel 15, God instructed Saul through the prophet Samuel to destroy all the Amalekites and all their possessions. King Saul decided to destroy all the Amalekites except King Agag and the best of the livestock. King Saul's disobedience resulted in God rejecting him, and then an evil spirit entering.

> *"And Samuel said, Hath the Lord as great delight in burnt offerings and sacrifices, as in obeying the voice of the Lord? Behold, to obey is better than sacrifice, and to hearken than the fat of rams. For rebellion is as the sin of witchcraft, and stubbornness is as iniquity and idolatry. Because thou hast rejected the word of the Lord, he hath also rejected thee from being king." (1 Samuel 15:22-23)*

> *"But the Spirit of the Lord departed from Saul, and an evil spirit from the Lord troubled him." (1 Samuel 16:14)*

This scripture states that an evil Spirit *from the Lord* troubled Saul. You may be questioning whether God sends demons into people. That answer is of course not! The term "from the Lord" can be interpreted as *permitted by the Lord*. Your next question may be why did God allow an evil spirit to enter Saul? The answer is because he was disobedient to God's word.

> It is critical that if you fall, you repent and turn away from that sin immediately so that you can be restored.

When you are in disobedience, there is a possibility that demons can enter. Because the Kingdom of God is a kingdom, it is governed by laws. When these laws are violated, demons may have the legal right to enter. Do demons enter every time a believer falls into sin, or are not following God's word? I do not believe so. According to scripture, King Saul was unrepentant, which opened the door for demons to enter. In my opinion, King David sinned worse than King Saul. He committed adultery and murder, but you never read where an evil spirit entered David. I believe this is because David repented. When the prophet Samuel confronted King Saul, he lied and made excuses. When the prophet Nathan confronted David, he repented.

> *"And David said unto Nathan, I have sinned against the Lord. And Nathan said unto David, The Lord also hath put away thy sin; thou shalt not die." (2 Samuel 12:13)*

David's prayer of repentance:

> *"Create in me a clean heart, O God; and renew a right spirit within me. Cast me not away from thy presence; and take not thy holy spirit from me. Restore unto me the joy of thy salvation; and uphold me with thy free spirit." (Psalm 51:10-11)*

Even though David suffered consequences for his sins, he was not demonized like King Saul due to his repentance. David was able to make a full recovery, and God called him a man after his own heart. What we can glean from this is that unconfessed sins cause demons to enter in. It is critical that if you fall, you repent and turn away from that sin immediately so that you can be restored. It is not God's will for you to be demonized, but if you are out of alignment with God's word, then you are exposing yourself.

One of the most powerful things you can walk a person through before inner healing and deliverance is repentance. There was a member of a church that I pastored that constantly desired prayer because of a physical affliction that crippled her. She would limp to the altar, I would pray for her, she would get totally healed, and walk away normal. What bothered me was that she would come back to the altar with the same condition within two to three weeks. Finally, I asked the Holy Spirit what was going on, and he revealed to me that she had a spirit of infirmity that was connected to a man she was having sex with who was not her husband. She would get healed but then sleep with him again, and that spirit would just come back. After inquiring with her about what I was feeling, she surprisingly acknowledged that it was true. The problem was not the demon. For her to get delivered and stay free, she needed to stop having sex with that man.

There was another member that I prayed for because she was tormented by demons of depression, suicide, and low self-esteem. She would cough, choke, vomit, scream, and be totally free. Her freedom lasted for a week or two, at best. Then I would receive a call with her on the phone crying, "Pastor, it's back. I keep hearing that I'm nothing and I'm better off dead and I want to kill myself. I'm so sad." Finally, after her third deliverance session, the Holy Spirit told me not to pray for her anymore because the issue was not the demon but her lack of faith and obedience to God's word. Instead of believing what God's word says, she believed what that demon was telling her about herself. In my book, *God Therapy*, I share my story of how I battled with a demon of depression. Part of me getting free and staying free was that I broke my partnership with those negative beliefs about who I was. I began to accept and confess who God said I was, which caused the demon to lose its legal right and grip on my mind and emotions. I have been free for over twenty years. This brings me to the next reason Christians become demonized.

NEGATIVE BELIEF SYSTEM

> *"Finally, brethren, whatsoever things are true, whatsoever things are honest, whatsoever things are just, whatsoever things are pure, whatsoever things are lovely, whatsoever things are of good report; if there be any virtue, and if there be any praise, think on these things." (Philippians 4:8)*

This verse is to instruct the believer about their thought life and what things you should think about. When you do not follow God's word regarding your thinking, you are out of alignment with his word, and it can open doors for demons to come in.

One of the main areas demons attack us is in our thought life. If the enemy can get you to partner with what he says, he can enter and gain control of that area of your life. We must remember that transformation begins in the mind. There is no use in trying to change your behavior without changing your thinking. Your negative thoughts empower demonic spirits. When you break your partnership with demonic messages, the demonic spirits attached to those thoughts are weakened and their power over that area of your life can be broken.

I ministered to a lot of Christians who were demonized by a spirit of depression and low self-esteem. They acted depressed, and they felt depressed because of depressing thoughts about themselves or their life. This resulted in an open door for the demon of depression to enter. For them to get totally free, they had to change the way they thought about themselves. If the truth makes you free according to John 8:32, believing a lie causes bondage. It is not good enough to renounce the lie or negative thought, you must replace it with the truth or a healthy thought. I call this replacement therapy. If you renounce without replacing the belief system, the negative belief has space to return along with the demonic spirits connected to it. The moment it is replaced, it gives no room for the negative belief to reenter. I will go deeper into this later on and give you steps on how to heal your thoughts or what I call stinking thinking.

RESILIENCY THOROUGH SPIRITUALITY

> *"Finally, my brethren, be strong in the Lord, and in the power of his might. Put on the whole armour of God, that ye may be able to stand against the wiles of the devil." (Ephesians 6:10-11)*

According to this scripture, your stand is directly connected to your spiritual strength. To stand against the wiles or tricks of the devil, you must be strong in God. If you are weak in God, then you become vulnerable and demonic spirits can gain access. All of us as believers have weak moments but it is important not to stay there. Just because you have a weak moment does not mean that you are weak. Just because you have a sad moment does not mean that you are depressed. However, if you stay in that state, then what is on you will get in you, and you will become the thing you are dealing with. The key to being strong in the Lord is through consistently seeking God. It is impossible to seek God and stay in a state of weakness. Neglecting your spiritual responsibilities to pray, read your Bible, and be faithful to your local church causes you to become spiritually weak.

> Just like we take care of our natural bodies, we must take care of our spiritual bodies. Just like we can be full naturally, it is our Christian responsibility to stay full of the Holy Spirit.

The Bible tells us that the devil is like a roaring lion. "Be sober, be vigilant; because your adversary the devil, as a *roaring lion*, walketh about, seeking whom he may devour." (1 Peter 5:8) I recall watching a documentary about a family of lions. In this documentary, there was a herd of about 1,000 buffalo grazing in a field. What was interesting was that the lions did not attack the buffalo but were observing them. They scrutinized the buffaloes because they were looking for a particular one. I thought they were looking for the most enormous, meatiest buffalo. If I were a lion that is what I would do. To my surprise, they were looking for the weakest one. They were looking for one that was crippled, immature, or had wandered off from the safety of the herd. When they found that one, they ran past all the other buffaloes – some being just feet away – to get to that weak one. That is how the devil works. He looks for weak areas in your life so that he can gain access. According to Jude 1:20, it is our responsibility to keep ourselves built up in God. We stay built up through praying in tongues or praying in our heavenly language. Praying in tongues or your heavenly prayer language is one of the most powerful tools a Christian must utilize to stay strong.

THE IMPORTANCE OF PRAYING IN TONGUES

"A person who speaks in tongues is strengthened personally…" (1 Corinthians 14:4 NLT)

When we pray in tongues as the *"Spirit gives utterance"* (Acts 2:4), we are supernaturally built up or strengthened by the Holy Spirit. I remember having a long, draining day at work and going to church physically tired, emotionally drained, and mentally depleted. I had to teach Bible study that day, and I did not feel like teaching. Before Bible study, we traditionally knelt on our knees and prayed. As I knelt, I felt the presence of God come upon me, and I began to pray in tongues. I was astonished that when I stood up, my physical tiredness was gone, emotionally I felt reinvigorated, and mentally I felt awakened. This is because as I was praying in my heavenly language, the Holy Spirit was strengthening me and pouring into me.

Just like we take care of our natural bodies, we must take care of our spiritual bodies. Just like we can be full naturally, it is our Christian responsibility to stay full of the Holy Spirit. Praying in tongues is not something we should do occasionally or religiously. It is something we are instructed to do daily.

> "Praying always with all prayer and supplication in the Spirit..."
> (Ephesians 6:18)

Praying always in our heavenly language ensures that we stay spiritually fit and strong in God. Praying in tongues is also an excellent coping mechanism because it releases God's presence which causes the feel-good neurotransmitter – dopamine – to be released in our mind and emotions. It is common that after you pray in tongues for a while, your countenance changes, and you begin to feel happy, motivated, encouraged, and at peace.

Praying in tongues keeps us resilient and allows us to bounce back when circumstances occur in our life that causes us to become discouraged, depressed, or afraid. Praying in tongues keeps us full of the Holy Spirit which keeps demonic spirits out. When something is full, nothing else can get in.

If you have never spoken in tongues, the Bible shares with you that it is a gift given because of your relationship with Jesus Christ. It's not something that man gives you, it comes straight from heaven. It is also given to those who are obedient to God's word and ask Father God for it. One evidence that you have been filled with the Holy Spirit is speaking in your heavenly language. Here are some scriptures:

> *"I indeed baptize you with water unto repentance: but he that cometh after me is mightier than I, whose shoes I am not worthy to bear: he shall baptize you with the Holy Ghost, and with fire:" (Matthew 3:11)*

> *"The God of our fathers raised up Jesus, whom ye slew and hanged on a tree. Him hath God exalted with his right hand to be a Prince and a Saviour, for to give repentance to Israel, and forgiveness of sins. And we are his witnesses of these things; and so is also the Holy Ghost, whom God hath given to them that obey him." (Acts 5: 30-32)*

> *"And I say unto you, Ask, and it shall be given you; seek, and ye shall find; knock, and it shall be opened unto you. For every one that asketh receiveth; and he that seeketh findeth; and to him that knocketh it shall be opened. If a son shall ask bread of any of you that is a father, will he give him a stone? or if he ask a fish, will he for a fish give him a serpent? Or if he shall ask an egg, will he offer him a scorpion? If ye then, being evil, know how to give good gifts unto your children: how much more shall your heavenly Father give the Holy Spirit to them that ask him?" (Luke 11:9-13)*

> *"And they were all filled with the Holy Ghost, and began to speak with other tongues, as the Spirit gave them utterance." (Acts 2:4)*

Speaking in your heavenly language is not difficult. It is something that Father God gives you because of your relationship with Jesus Christ. The scriptures states that as they spoke the Spirit gave them utterance. All you must do is speak and the Spirit will begin to provide you with the utterance. Most of the time you can feel the energy, presence, or power of the Holy Spirit inside of you while you're speaking. It is a supernatural, surreal experience that's difficult to articulate. One of the results is that you feel more joy and peace and more connected to God.

CHANGING YOUR BELIEF SYSTEM

According to the cognitive-behavioral therapy theory, your belief system is the control tower for your emotions and behavior. Change must take place in the mind before it takes place in the emotions or behavior. One of the most powerful ways to address distorted messages is through hearing the voice of God.

> *"Then they cry unto the Lord in their trouble, and he saveth them out of their distresses. He sent his word, and healed them, and delivered them from their destructions." (Psalm 107:19-20)*

According to this scripture, hearing the voice of God brings healing and deliverance. I have had a myriad of sessions where a person was severely wounded and tormented by belief systems of "It's my fault," "I'm not good enough," "I'm not lovable," and "God has forsaken me." During these sessions, I would ask my clients to picture Jesus, express to him their belief system, and ask him what the truth is. Then I would ask them what they "sense, hear, or feel Jesus is saying." Suddenly with their eyes closed, their tormented, sad countenance would change, and they would begin to weep as Jesus Christ began to speak to them. As they shared with me what he was saying to them, I could literally see the power of God fulfilling Psalm 107:20—healing and delivering them through his word.

DESTROYING DEMONIC STRONGHOLDS

> *"(For the weapons of our warfare are not carnal, but mighty through God to the pulling down of strong holds;) Casting down imaginations, and every high thing that exalteth itself against the knowledge of God, and bringing into captivity every thought to the obedience of Christ;"* (2 Corinthians 10:4)

A stronghold is a fortified city – massive wall structures – kingdoms used to keep their opponent from entering in, defeating them, and dispossessing them. According to this scripture, a demonic stronghold is an "imagination" or a belief system. When a person is partnering with a demon in their belief system, it creates a stronghold causing the individual to be in bondage to their opposing beliefs. To cast out the demon, the stronghold must first be broken. This means that before you cast the demon out, the belief system connected to the demon has to be identified and destroyed. A deliverance minister cannot do this for you. You must willingly repent and renounce the negative belief system and accept what God's word has to say. A person ministering to you can share with you the word of God, but it is not effective unless you accept it and break your partnership with the demonic message, which gives the demon legal right to be there.

Chapter 11

The Benefits & Limitations of Therapy

There is a clinical approach to addressing trauma, and I am a firm believer in therapy. As a therapist, I have been able to support countless Christian and non-Christians with the emotional and mental challenges they were facing. My therapeutic experience was a crucial component in developing *God Therapy* and *Advanced God Therapy Inner Healing and Deliverance Treatment Models*. I would not be a clinical therapist if I did not believe in it. I have encountered Christians and Christian leaders speaking against working with a therapist. As a believer growing up in an African American church, I was culturally and religiously led to believe that I was weak and lacked faith if I saw a therapist. I honestly believe that I would have resolved my challenges sooner if I sought therapeutic assistance.

Going to therapy does not minimize your relationship with God or your Christian stance. I am a firm believer that until you receive total healing, you need all the support you can get. Clinicians are trained in evidence-based methods to help you to improve. If you feel that what you are dealing with is beyond your capacity to control, you should seek therapeutic help. I have had clients with severe trauma that the power of Jesus Christ has totally healed through my inner healing and deliverance method. I have also had clients that received a level of healing. Some I have recommended seeing a therapist to continue their process of healing and learn tools to cope with their problems. Inner healing and deliverance are a short-term intervention. If need be, an individual can see a mental health counselor to receive long-term support.

Going to therapy does not minimize your relationship with God or your Christian stance.

BENEFITS OF MENTAL HEALTH COUNSELING

1. Teach you healthy coping skills and self-soothing techniques which will assist you with managing symptoms such as depression, anger, anxiety, and stress.
2. Build self-awareness and emotional intelligence.
3. Help you process the traumatic event and assist with cognitive restructuring.
4. Assist you with finding resources and developing a support system.
5. Provide medication from a psychiatrist to assist with managing your symptoms.

Having said that, therapy has its limitations. Most clinical theories state that there is no healing for disorders connected to trauma. The treatment of trauma is a long-term process that requires years of therapeutic methodologies. In many cases, you are also provided with medication to support you around coping with the mental and emotional symptoms of trauma. You will be assisted with managing your symptoms, but most clinical therapists are led to believe that there is no cure for most mental and emotional disorders. This may lead you to believe that you must carry the diagnoses or labels for the rest of your life. Also, seeing a therapist does not address the spiritual component of trauma, which is demonization. Most people who have been traumatized are demonized because the act and impact of trauma open doors for demons to enter. When a demon enters a person, the symptoms of what a person is dealing with are amplified. Therefore, trauma must be addressed not just from a mental or emotional level but also from a spiritual level.

Chapter 12

The Benefits & Limitations of the Church

I have literally attended church my entire life. Both my grandfather and father were pastors. Growing up, I was required to be in church for just about every service. At the age of eighteen, I gave my life to Christ. I loved going to church, and the key to my growth and development as a Christian was my faithfulness to the church. Throughout my life, I have probably served in every position in the church. I served as a musician, greeter, deacon, board member, youth leader, choir member, janitor, Bible teacher, and even a senior pastor. I love church and believe in the church.

As a pastor, I have a conviction about making sure people understand the importance of being faithful to their local church. However, attending church services does not usually heal trauma. Many are being preached to and prayed for but aren't being healed. Countless people are sitting in church service after service, they may feel better, but they are not delivered from the effect of trauma. Their spiritual growth is being stunted due to not directly dealing with their problems. Their souls are saved, but other parts are still fractured, because just attending church does not allow them to address their inner healing and deliverance needs adequately.

Pastors and leaders are quitting the ministry, and some have committed suicide because they lacked proper therapy to address their hidden struggles. How they present themselves in the pulpit is different from how they really are in private. Christians are falling, not because of a lack of church, but a lack of counsel.

"Where no counsel is, the people fall: But in the multitude of counsellors there is safety." (Proverbs 11:14)

The church is beneficial, but some people need church *and* counseling. Here are the benefits and limitations of the church.

BENEFITS OF CHURCH ATTENDANCE

- Pastoral care and other church resources should provide a loving community, spiritual education, and support. This assists with the social and spiritual needs of an individual which enhances their quality of life. This also assists with the healing process.
- Preaching and teaching can help a person feel better, address negative beliefs, develop spiritually, and assist with the healing process.
- Prayer ministry can assist with the healing process and bring relief from trauma.

LIMITATIONS OF TRADITIONAL CHURCH

- Preaching, prayer, and traditional church services alone do not usually heal trauma.
- Addressing trauma usually requires one-on-one support.
- Healing trauma usually requires treatment not just teaching or preaching.
- Most ministers are not trained in the proper techniques, treatment, and procedures to heal trauma.

This may be alarming to some, so allow me to share scripture to support what I am saying. According to Mark 4:13-20, people who are preached to have a 25% chance of being impacted by the word of God. In this parable, the sower represents the preacher, teacher, pastor or whoever is speaking the word of God. The seed represents the word of God. The soil represents the person that's receiving the word of God.

> *"The sower soweth the word. And these are they by the way side, where the word is sown; but when they have heard, Satan cometh immediately, and taketh away the word that was sown in their hearts. And these are they likewise which are sown on stony ground; who, when they have heard the word, immediately receive it with gladness; and have no root in themselves, and so endure but for a time: afterward, when affliction or persecution ariseth for the word's sake, immediately they are offended. And these are they which are sown among thorns; such as hear the word, and the cares of this world, and the deceitfulness of riches, and the lusts of other things entering in, choke the word, and it becometh unfruitful. And these are they which are sown on good ground; such as hear the word, and receive it, and bring forth fruit, some thirtyfold, some sixty, and some an hundred." (Mark 4:15-20)*

The word of God is infallible and potent. It has the supernatural aptitude to heal, deliver, and set free anyone from any dilemma or trauma. According to this scripture, the issue is not the word of God (the seed) or the person teaching the word (the sower); the problem lies with the person receiving the word of God (the soil). The word cannot penetrate because the individual is not receiving it properly. Three things happen to cause the word of God not be effective: Satan comes and takes the word away; affliction causes an individual not to be able to retain the word; or the cares of this world and the lusts of other things takes priority over the word. If a person properly receives the word of God, it will bring forth fruit, but according to the parable of the sower, this occurs in a ratio of 1 in 4 which is 25% of individuals. These statistics are alarming.

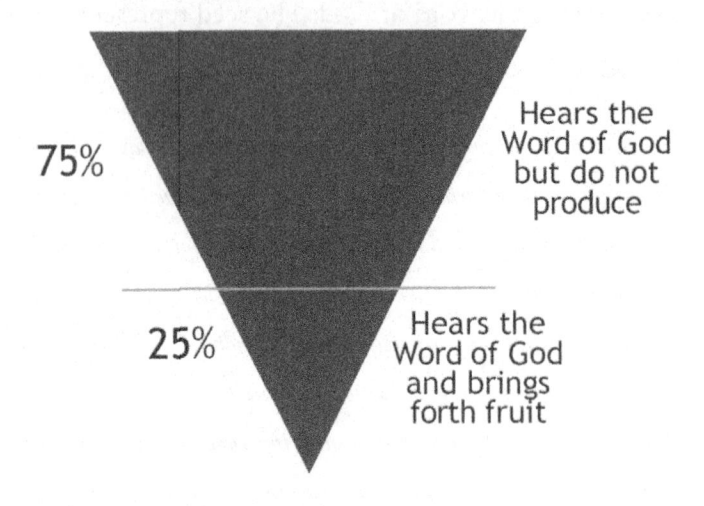

```
75%  — Hears the Word of God but do not produce
25%  — Hears the Word of God and brings forth fruit
```

Can you imagine that the word of God does not transform 75 percent of the people in your church? They may shout, dance, clap their hands, and say "amen," but internally there's no shift. There's no healing or deliverance. This would be okay if the purpose of the word of God was to make you happy and have an emotional experience, but this is not the case. The purpose of the word of God is to bring change, transformation, and healing. "He sent his word, and healed them, And delivered them from their destructions" (Psalms 107:20). These statistics are worse where there are churches who are not preaching the true gospel. There's a difference between a good message and the true gospel. When the true gospel is preached, souls are saved and people are challenged to change.

> "For I am not ashamed of the gospel of Christ: for it is the power of God unto salvation to everyone that believeth; to the Jew first, and also to the Greek." (Romans 1:16)

When it comes to healing trauma in our churches, can you imagine the number of wounded people who are worshipping, coming to service after service, being taught the Bible but still broken. How do we fix this? To resolve this issue, churches should have ministry teams or Christian counselors that are properly trained and equipped to specifically bring inner healing and deliverance from trauma. By applying the word of God with the proper healing strategies, people can be totally free from the mental and emotional damage and demonization that comes from trauma. It is not fair or possible for a pastor to carry this burden alone because of the demand on a pastor to oversee the entire church functionality. In my *God Therapy Training Academy*, I train ministries and churches on proper techniques and structures to set in place to address these needs.

HINDERANCES TO HEALING

Many people do not get healed and wonder why it is not happening for them. Various blockages can hinder the healing process. One of those issues is unconfessed sin. James wrote to the church and let them know that they had to confess their faults or their sins if they wanted to be healed.

> *"Confess your faults one to another, and pray one for another, that ye may be healed. The effectual fervent prayer of a righteous man availeth much." (James 5:16)*

When a person neglects to confess and acknowledge their flaws, it blocks the healing process. They are not being healed because they still carry unforgiveness, bitterness, pride, anger, etc. One of my favorite quotes is from Hippocrates. He said, "Before you heal someone, ask him if he's willing to give up the things that make him sick." To be healed, a person must be willing to confess and forsake those things that are causing them to become sick. Remember, the deeper issue is not that you are ill, the real problem is what is keeping you ill. The more significant matter is not that you are bound, it is what is hindering you from getting set free. You – not the devil or the people that hurt you – can be your greatest hindrance. It is your responsibility to get the help that you need so that you can be whole. There are resources and professionals that can assist you with your issue. There are spiritual leaders that God has anointed and assigned to walk you through to freedom. There are pastors that God has entrusted to shepherd you to health. Your job is to find them and work with them until you are completely whole.

The power of God is available to set you free, but you must remember that God works *with* us not *for* us. He cannot help you if you're not willing to do the work to help yourself. There is always a solution to a problem. You can complain about it, play the victim, or take action so that you can get the freedom you need. The Bible says faith without works is dead (James 2:26). Your healing and deliverance requires you to do something. It may be to pick up the phone and make a call to get help. It may be to commit to going to sessions. It may be making changes in how you think or act. Whatever it is, you must be willing to do the work so that you can become whole. God has given you the ability; you have to take action.

> *"Now unto him that is able to do exceeding abundantly above all that we ask or think, according to the power that worketh in us" (Ephesians 3:20).*

> To be healed, a person must be willing to confess and forsake those things that are causing them to become sick.

Everyone has a warrior and a wimp inside of them. If you give in to the wimp, you will run away from your issues, hurt and pain, and never be free. If you tap into the warrior in you, you will fight through any challenge and draw on the power inside of you to overcome what's coming against you. Think about the woman with the issue of blood. Even though she was physically, emotionally, and mentally drained from dealing with her issue for twelve years, she was willing to do whatever it took to get her healing. She found Jesus, pressed through the crowd, and got her healing. She didn't have the strength to touch anything else, so with the bit of strength she had left, she touched his garment.

> *"And, behold, a woman, which was diseased with an issue of blood twelve years, came behind him, and touched the hem of his garment: for she said within herself, If I may but touch his garment, I shall be whole. But Jesus turned him about, and when he saw her, he said, Daughter, be of good comfort; thy faith hath made thee whole. And the woman was made whole from that hour." (Matthew 9:20-22)*

You must have a "whatever it takes" attitude. Whatever it takes, I am going to get my healing. Whatever it takes, I am going to get my blessing. Whatever it takes, I am going to get my breakthrough. I have seen people healed from the worst cases, and I can take no credit for it. It was because of their perseverance and determination to do whatever it took to get to Jesus so they could be healed. It was their desperation to stick to the process so that they could be totally free. They allowed me to walk with them to those deepest, darkest places of trauma so they could experience healing and deliverance. Whatever they had to do, they did it so that they could be liberated from things that tormented them for years. If they can do it, you can do it too. God is no respecter of person, and no one is better than another. It is about having the fortitude to move forward to your freedom. You must have the resolve that you will not give up until you get what God has for you, which is healing, deliverance, and breakthrough.

> *To be healed, a person must be willing to confess and forsake those things that are causing them to become sick.*

THE MAIN COMPONENTS FOR HEALING TRAUMA

One of the most important steps to healing trauma is forgiveness and repentance. You must come to the place where you are willing to forgive the person who hurt you and repent from any bitterness, hatred, anger, or revenge you may be carrying. "Vengeance is mine; I will repay, saith the Lord" (Romans 12:19a). Unforgiveness blocks God for entering into the healing process.

After forgiveness has taken place, you can invite Jesus to come and heal that broken part of you that has been damaged by the trauma. True repentance is not just telling God you are sorry. That is the religious way of repentance. True repentance is confessing and forsaking sin. Acts 3:19 states that in order for your sins to be forgiven you must repent and convert, which is to turn away from sin. This may be a shock to your religious system, but God does not forgive you because you say you are sorry. If you are not willing to turn away from what you are sorry about, then you are not genuinely sorry.

> *"He that covereth his sins shall not prosper: But whoso confesseth and forsaketh them shall have mercy" (Proverbs 28:13).*

Chapter 13

Methods to Healing Trauma God's Way

God's will is not for his people to carry inner wounds and demonization. His desire is for us to be totally healed and whole. As stated before, giving your life to Jesus Christ does not automatically heal the trauma. Salvation saves us from sin and the penalty of sin (Matthew 1:21, Romans 6:23), but physical or emotional healing is not automatic. Christ's work on the cross is more than receiving him as Lord and Savior. In addition to salvation, Christians must experience healing and deliverance.

> "But upon mount Zion shall be deliverance, and there shall be holiness; and the house of Jacob shall possess their possessions." (Obadiah 1:17)

> "Then Philip went down to the city of Samaria, and preached Christ unto them. And the people with one accord gave heed unto those things which Philip spake, hearing and seeing the miracles which he did. For unclean spirits, crying with loud voice, came out of many that were possessed with them: and many taken with palsies, and that were lame, were healed. And there was great joy in that city." (Acts 8:5-8)

There are four stages to healing trauma: encountering Jesus, healing the emotions, a changed belief system, and casting out demons.

THE ENCOUTNER WITH CHRIST

> *"Behold, I stand at the door, and knock: if any man hear my voice, and open the door, I will come in to him, and will sup with him, and he with me." (Revelation 3:20)*

Not only does he desire an intimate relationship with you, but he also wants to heal your hurt.

Jesus does not come where he is not invited. You can invite Jesus in certain areas of your life and leave him out of others. Some Christians experience Jesus on a religious level, but Jesus is much more than just a religious experience. Not only does he desire an intimate relationship with you, but he also wants to heal your hurt. When Jesus says, "Behold, I stand at the door and knock," I believe Jesus is speaking of the door to your heart. When we experience traumatic situations, we subconsciously put-up walls for the purpose of not allowing anybody into the fragmented places of our hearts. The issue with this is not only do we shut people out, but we shut Jesus out, too. When it comes to other people, we cannot let everybody into the most sensitive and fragile places of our hearts. Everyone cannot be trusted, and everyone does not have the capacity or skill to handle your trauma. There must be a level of reliability, acceptance, and love before people are allowed into those places.

However, when it comes to letting Jesus in, he has already proven that we can trust him and that he loves and accepts us unconditionally. Jesus desires to come into the broken areas of your heart so that he can love on you and release the curative power of his presence. Too many

Christians stay bound, wounded, and demonized, not because Jesus does not want to heal them, but because they are not allowing him to come into those broken areas.

When King David committed adultery and murder, he got right back on the throne as if nothing happened. We all have the propensity to attempt to go on with our lives and pretend nothing has happened. Nathan, the prophet, forced David to face what he was trying to avoid, and through his encounter with the truth, he was able to receive restoration. Jesus is the truth (John 14:16)! Inner healing happens when we experience or encounter Jesus at the point of our pain, guilt, shame, fear, or rejection. When we allow him in, Jesus promises the following:

> *"For the scripture saith, whosoever believeth on him shall not be ashamed. For there is no difference between the Jew and the Greek: for the same Lord over all is rich unto all that call upon him. For whosoever shall call upon the name of the Lord shall be saved." (Romans 10:11-13)*

This scripture is usually only used for the salvation of the soul, but in Greek, *saved* means healed, preserved, rescued. Just like you called on him to save your soul, you need to call on him to heal your mind and emotions. Just like you had an encounter with Jesus to free you from sin, you need an encounter with Jesus to free you from your trauma. This is important because when a person experiences trauma, there are traumatic images imprinted in a person's psyche. The traumatic pictures cause the person to continue to experience the symptoms connected to the trauma. Encountering Christ at the point of the trauma releases a supernatural imprint of God's healing presence and power. Jesus comes in and changes the narrative and allows you to experience the trauma with him in it healing you.

> Jesus desires to come into the broken areas of your heart so that he can love on you and release the curative power of his presence.

In my inner healing and deliverance therapy sessions, I facilitate my clients through a process of inviting Jesus to heal their wounds at the point of the traumatic event. What usually happens is they begin to have real encounters with Jesus. They literally feel, sense, hear, or see him healing the area within them that's been traumatized. Some even begin to have visions of Jesus. This mental healing occurs because the traumatic images of what happened are replaced with the healed images or encounters of Jesus's comfort and love.

I had a client that was afraid to get into cars. Anytime she would get into a car she would have a full-blown panic attack. Her heart would begin to pulsate, she would breathe heavily, and curl up while screaming and crying. I walked her through a process where I had her visualize herself in the car. She began to experience the symptoms like she normally does, and she said she sees herself in the back seat crying and screaming in fear. Then I had her picture Jesus in the car with her, and we invited him to heal her. Suddenly, her breathing slowed down, and she saw Jesus in the car comforting and protecting her. She said she could hear him telling her that she is safe and that he is with her every time she gets in a car. She then saw herself in the front seat looking out the window. While smiling, she told me how beautiful the scenery was and how she realized how much she has been missing because of fear.

PAIN IS NOT THE PROBLEM

Pain is not your problem, but what's causing the pain is. Pain is the body sensation of discomfort or hurt. It is an unpleasant and usually unwanted sensory experience. Would you believe it if I told you that God created painful emotions? Yes, pain is not from the devil; it's from God. I will take it even further, not only is pain from God, but pain is not bad. What caused the pain may be harmful or even demonic, but pain itself is not bad – it's natural. Let me reiterate, there is a difference between creating something and causing something. God created pain, but God does not usually cause pain. It is brought about because of the decisions and actions of people who are generally demonically motivated. It can be caused by the decisions we make that are harmful to ourselves. Finally, pain is a natural process of life. Whatever the source of the pain, pain has a God-given purpose and plan. Pain is your body's way of communicating that something is wrong so that you can attend to it. It lets you know that something hurtful is happening.

If you put your hand on a hot stove, imagine what would happen to you if you did not feel pain. Yes, it would cause more damage because your brain would not get the message to remove your hand. Pain is your body's way of getting your attention. Pain is your body's GPS to let you know there is an issue and where it is located. If you follow pain, you will find the root problem. Pain is your body's alarm system. Just like your house has alarm systems such as fire alarms, carbon monoxide detectors, or burglar alarms, pain is your alarm system. It causes unpleasant feelings to solicit a response from you to bring all the resources to that area to fix what is wrong. Pain's job is to tell you there's a problem, and your job is to fix the problem that pain is presenting. Instead of trying to avoid it, you need to notice it, name it and do something about it.

Healing happens when you resolve the issues that pain is presenting. This causes the pain to subside. Pain is not meant to be silenced. You must allow pain to speak and express itself and then give it the proper nurture, care, and support. Since most people think pain is bad, we run away from it instead of trying understanding and resolving it. If you learn to listen to the pain, you can gain a lot of wisdom about what's going on inside of you and what you need to do to stay healthy. When pain is ignored, the issue worsens, and you can become more confused about the essence of the painful experience. Problems are created when pain is not appropriately managed.

You Do Not Need All the Answers

Plenty of people who are carrying inner wounds have unanswered questions and wonder why. Why did they do this or why did they do that or why did God allow this to happen? For inner healing to take place, you do not need an answer to these questions. You must allow yourself space to release the pain connected to the why and accept that somethings you will never understand or receive an answer to. Acceptance is a part of the healing process. Sometimes, Jesus will give you understanding and revelation to answer your why, or as life goes on, you gain a greater understanding as to why. Other times you might not receive an answer. Closure happens by either obtaining a solution to unanswered questions or through acceptance of the fact that you might never understand. Healing doesn't require you to understand everything; you can move forward without having all the facts.

Cry It Out

Another component necessary for inner healing to take place is catharsis. Most people carry inner wounds because they have never released the pain connected to what has been done to them. Unreleased hurt causes an emotional buildup of hurt, shame, guilt, anger, sadness, and fear. Eventually you will become so overwhelmed that you will explode, implode, or shut down and become numb. Releasing this pain is like letting air out of a balloon. You receive relief through release.

I remember when I was called to go to a middle school in the inner city of Chicago to do crisis counseling. One of the student's brother was shot and killed right across the street from the school during school hours. Many of the students saw the body lying in the middle of the road. When I arrived at the school the following day, I saw the blood residue still on the street. What shocked me the most is that the parent allowed the child whose brother was murdered to come to school the next day, and teachers seemed desensitized and carried on as usual.

I sat in a room with at least forty students, and I gave them a safe space to express their pain in a loving, supportive environment. The boy whose brother was killed sat next to me. These seventh and eighth graders began to cry, grieve, and talk about what they had experienced growing up in a community inundated with violence and gang activity. By the time the session was over, the students had smiles on their faces and expressed that they felt better and felt like a weight was lifted off them. They wanted me to come back weekly. All I did was gave them space to express their pain and cry so that they could experience catharsis. One of the most effective ways to release pain is through crying. The writers in the book of Psalms, including King David, constantly demonstrated this:

"In my distress I cried unto the Lord, and he heard me." (Psalm 120:1)

"Out of the depths have I cried unto thee, O Lord." (Psalm 130:1)

"In the day when I cried, thou answeredst me, and strengthenedst me with strength in my soul." (Psalm 138:3)

Even Jesus demonstrated releasing his pain through crying. There are four times the Bible mentions Jesus crying:

> *Jesus cried when he came to see Lazarus in the grave. (John 11:35)*
>
> *He cried when he saw Jerusalem and the spiritual condition it was in. (Luke 19: 41-42)*
>
> *He cried in the Garden of Gethsemane because of the agony of facing the cross. (Luke 22:44)*
>
> *He cried while on the cross because of the pain he was enduring. (Mark 15:33)*

Notice in these scriptures that these were all men who cried. One of the reasons why some men have a hard time expressing their emotions is that they were taught not to cry as young boys. This is not just an issue with men, some cultures and families teach us not to cry – that crying makes you weak. On the contrary, not crying makes you vulnerable because the hurt and pain sit inside of you and becomes toxic. Crying is an important part of the healing process, and it helps us release pain and pent-up emotions. It is true that you cannot cry in front of everybody. It would be best if you had a safe environment where you can allow yourself to cry liberally and release the pain. This can be with a trusted friend, minister, counselor, or by yourself. There are many benefits of crying.

Here are some of them:
- Brings healing naturally.
- Acts as a soothing mechanism to the mind, body, and emotions.
- Releases hurt and decreases stress.
- Eliminates toxins from the body.
- Releases chemicals that make you feel good after you have cried.

- Assists with the grieving process so that you can grieve, gain closure, and move forward.
- Brings God's blessings, comfort, and love. Matthew 5:4 states, *"Blessed are they that mourn: for they shall be comforted."*

GETTING PAST THE PAST

When you experience trauma, a part of you becomes disjointed and emotionally stuck. Even though the trauma is over and time has elapsed, the pain connected to the trauma still lives. The trauma constantly gets sparked and you experience an emotional time travel. In other words, the pain of what happened resurfaces and you feel like you felt when it first happened. I had a client who was having parenting challenges. During the session she began to say how she feels "stupid" and "inadequate." After the episode was over, I asked her where those feelings come from. She told me that she grew up with a verbally abusive mother who told her those things. When circumstances arose, those negative feelings constantly resurfaced and caused her to feel like she felt when she was a child.

Healing trauma can be challenging because trauma causes the wounds to be tattooed to your emotions or psyche. With psychotherapy, it can take years to experience healing. But Jesus, being the word of God, has the power to heal and transform those wounds in a moment. During God Therapy sessions the anointing is used to destroy the yokes of trauma and bring healing to the mind, body, soul and spirit. It's not just a clinical process, it's a supernatural process that expedites your healing. I'm not saying that all healing is instant. Certainly not, it is usually a progression; but I've seen Father God also work instantly and totally heal suddenly. Yes, we serve a God of suddenly and you can never underestimate the power of God to set you free.

FREEDOM FROM STINKING THINKING

The reason why the children of Israel could not go into the promise land is, not because they didn't have the capacity, they didn't have the mentality.

> *"But the men who had gone up with him said, "We are not able to go against the people. They are too strong for us… We looked like grasshoppers in our own eyes, and we looked the same to them" (Numbers 13: 31-33).*

The issue was not how others perceived them, but the negative view they had of themselves. I remember sitting in a training session with a group of male counselors. As my turn approached to speak, I began having an anxiety attack. My hands were sweating, my heart was beating fast, and I felt extremely nervous and fearful. I did not want to speak but wanted to skip my turn. I knew this was a problem because this was not the first time this happened. In fact, every time I sat in circles like this one with male therapists, I would have these anxiety attacks.

This time, I decided to trace my feelings and identify the stinking thinking that was driving my fear. While another therapist was talking and it was getting closer to my turn, I was doing my inner work tracing the emotion to find the message. I asked myself, "When did you first feel like this?" As I sat there gazing at the ceiling in deep thought, my childhood came up. I then realized that something happened to me in my childhood that caused me to be afraid of male authority figures. Then I thought, "What was the stinking thinking that I developed about myself that is connected to this childhood wound?" As I continued in my gaze, I realized the message connected to the emotion was that

"You are incompetent and no one cares about what you have to say." When it came my turn to speak, I stood up and shared my newfound discovery with the therapists. When I sat down, something therapeutic happened. Each therapist went around and shared with me that every time I speak, they are interested in what I have to say and that I carry a lot of wisdom and knowledge. As I was being validated, I felt something break within me, and it was like a warmth filled my heart. I then realized that the subconscious message was a lie and that I was competent. From that day forward, I never partnered with that message, and those anxiety attacks went away.

To heal the wound, restore your identity, and receive lasting deliverance, you must address your stinking thinking. What is the stinking thinking connected to your trauma that you have partnered with? I was able to be healed based on what man said to me. Imagine what would happen if you had an encounter with what Jesus has to say. Jesus says, "My sheep hear my voice, and I know them, and they follow me:" (John 10:27). The word hear means to know or to have a firm knowledge and conviction about. Jesus's desire is to speak to the wounded part of your heart that is carrying the wounded messages. When Jesus speaks to your heart, not only do you hear what he is saying, you feel what he is saying. Just like the wounded messages have pain connected to it, the healed messages Jesus speaks have peace, love, and joy attached to it. When the healed message from Jesus is imparted into your psyche and emotions, the wounded message is driven out along with the pain associated with it. When this happens, you are literally having an encounter with Jesus that's purifying your contaminated thoughts.

Below are examples of the wounded messages that people carry and the healed messages that are replaced once they experience inner healing.

Wounded Message vs Healed Message from Jesus

Wounded Message	Healed Message
I'm a failure.	You're not a failure. You have a future.
It's my fault.	It's not your fault; you were an innocent victim.
Nobody loves me.	I love you. You are loved.
I'm ugly.	I am beautiful, and God made me unique.
I can't ever . . .	If I put in the work, I can.
Things won't ever . . .	With God, all things are possible.

You are what you believe. In other words, your belief system impacts your identity. When it comes to deep level lasting inner healing and deliverance, prayer alone does not usually work. A person can receive prayer, but if they do not change their way of thinking, they may receive temporary relief, but the wound will remain.

I had a member whose friend died suddenly and unexpectedly. The moment she was told about it, she felt like she might die suddenly and unexpectedly. Consequently, she had a panic attack and had to be rushed to the hospital. From that moment forward, she suffered from panic attacks. She was under a therapist's care and was diagnosed and prescribed medicine. (As a side note, medication does not address the root issue. It is only a coping mechanism to control the symptoms.) For years, this individual was taking medication but never got healed from

Healing Trauma God's Way

the root cause of her panic attacks. She constantly came up for prayer, would get touched and feel better, but the panic attacks remained. I brought her in for a *God Therapy* session and God spoke to her telling her that she will live and not die. She felt the comfort of his presence and love and no longer accepted that stinking thinking. Afterward, I was able to cast out demonic spirits that were connected to her panic attacks. Through that encounter, she was totally healed, all symptoms ceased, and she was able to discontinue her medication.

As believers, it is important to stand in our authority and do what 2 Corinthians 10:5 says, *"Casting down imaginations, and every high thing that exalteth itself against the knowledge of God, and bringing into captivity every thought to the obedience of Christ..."* Once the mind is healed through the belief system being changed, then you are ready for deliverance.

> *"He that hath no rule over his own spirit is like a city that is broken down, and without walls." (Proverbs 25:28)*

You cannot allow your mind to control and dictate to you. You must control your mind. Your mind must be submitted to the word of God. If not, then you will be like a city that is broken down and without walls. That means that the enemy will come inside and there will be nothing to block him from entering. Demon spirits attack and attach to your thinking and emotions so that they can control your behavior. As soon as your thinking has been healed, demons lose their grip, authority, legal right, and they can easily be cast out.

CASTING OUT THE DEMONS

One of the impacts of trauma is demonization. The traumatic event opens the door for demon spirits to gain access to you. It is not just a mental or emotional issue; it is a spiritual issue. Going through deliverance alone usually does not cure trauma but is a component of the healing process. I had a session with a client who suffered from anxiety attacks and fear. She had been through deliverance before but kept finding herself demonized. The issue was not that she needed an exorcism, she needed to be educated. During the session, the gift of wisdom emerged and the Holy Spirit immediately gave me a download of what she needed to do to "manage, minimize, and master" her symptoms so that she could "maintain" her freedom. After the session, she was so excited and said, "That's just what I needed." The key to her healing was not deliverance. It was her going through inner healing and receiving tools to manage the fear and anxiety.

Even when it comes to deliverance, I have found that it does not take two to five hours or two to five days to cast out demonic spirits. It does not take two to three or more people to hold you down while the deliverance minister yells and screams to get a demon out. I believe more conservative churches have strayed away from deliverance because of deliverance being done incorrectly and the dramatics that some deliverance people use to free someone from a demon.

The Bible says let all things be done decently and in order (1 Corinthians 14:40). This includes deliverance too. When Jesus cast out demons, he simply commanded the spirits to come out, and they departed with minimal manifestations and without taking a long time. I have found that if you do the inner healing work before the deliverance, the spirit connected to the wound usually comes out within minutes and does not require screaming, restraining, using religious objects, or any other dramatics. You simply and assertively command the spirits to come out in Jesus's name, and they listen.

According to scripture, demons are subject to us through the name of Jesus Christ, "And the seventy returned again with joy, saying, Lord, even the devils are subject unto us through thy name" (Luke 10:17). The name of Jesus Christ alone is sufficient to cast out any devil. I recall as a young Christian being at a convention where leaders were casting a demon out of a young lady. I was shocked by what I was observing. The leaders were yelling, pushing, shaking, and at times, choking the young lady to free her from the demon. The more she manifested, the more aggressive they became. This is an inappropriate way to do deliverance work and can possibly do more damage to the person on the receiving end. Below is a picture that a client sent to me when her father (who was a pastor) attempted to do deliverance without addressing the damage. She shared with me that he started "yelling at the top of his lungs." The louder he became the more crazy and violent the manifestations. The person he was doing deliverance on started slithering on the floor and then ran into the bathroom and locked the door. As the father continued to yell my client shared with me what was happening behind the door, *"pastor it sounded like my cousin was being thrown around in the bathroom for like 30 min. straight and our bathroom was severely damaged."*

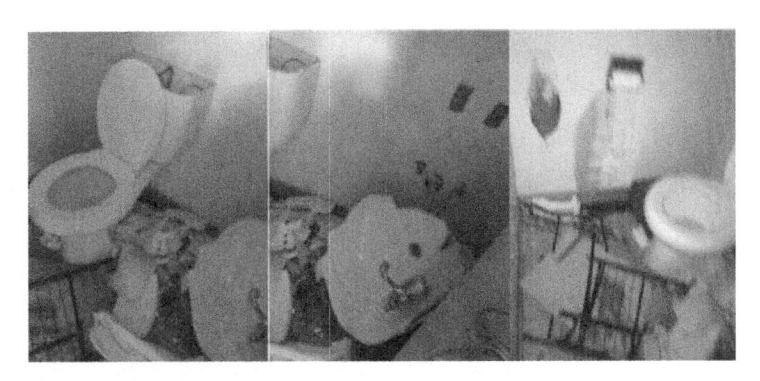

The actual pictures of the incidence that occurred in the bathroom.

KNOW WHAT YOU'RE DEALING WITH

Inner wounds, demonization, and sin are three different things that require three different approaches to be free of them. You get saved from sin (Matthew 1:21). You cannot cast out sin, and you cannot heal sin; you have to repent and forsake sin.

> *"Repent ye therefore, and be converted, that your sins may be blotted out, when the times of refreshing shall come from the presence of the Lord." (Acts 3:19)*

> *"He that covereth his sins shall not prosper: But whoso confesseth and forsaketh them shall have mercy." (Proverbs 28:13)*

As stated in 1 John 1:9, when you confess Jesus Christ as your Lord and savior, he forgives you and then saves you from sin.

According to Psalm 147:3, inner wounds must be healed. *"He healeth the broken in heart, and bindeth up their wounds."* These wounds are the mental and emotional damage caused by issues connected to trauma like abandonment, abuse, or childhood problems. If the internal issues are not addressed, it will spread externally. I believe one main reason why Christians are getting divorced, have broken families, and mental disorders are unaddressed heart wounds.

Deliverance was never meant to be complicated. What makes deliverance difficult is when people doing deliverance fail to deal with the sin, wounds, messages, and trauma the demons are connected to. Inner healing addresses these areas, and when these areas are addressed and the person has repented, received inner healing, and changed their beliefs, all you must do is simply command the demon to come out. Your deliverance is connected to your willingness to open your heart so that you can encounter Jesus, express and release the pain, forgive who you need to forgive, and break your partnership with the lies those demons are telling you. The moment this is done, demonic spirits are disarmed, dismantled, lose their legal right and can be easily cast out.

CAN YOU BE MADE WHOLE?

Healing is possible through the name of Jesus and the proper methods. Through faith in the name of Jesus Christ, there is supernatural power to bring healing to all manner of sickness and disease, whether mental, emotional, or physical.

> *"Wherefore God also hath highly exalted him, and given him a name which is above every name: That at the name of Jesus every knee should bow, of things in heaven, and things in earth, and things under the earth; And that every tongue should confess that Jesus Christ is Lord, to the glory of God the Father." (Philippians 2:9-11)*

It is important for you to understand that Jesus has purchased your healing on the cross. He was traumatized by the nails in his hands and nails in his feet so that you can be free from the impact of trauma. He carried the cross so that you would not have to carry the pains of this life. Although what happened is in the past, Jesus can revisit your past and remove the pain connected to your past memory. Here are some steps you can walk yourself through to invite Jesus to heal you from painful memories:

Note: I invite you to journal your experience.

- **Step 1:** Close your eyes and picture Jesus being with you. Picture the traumatic event and begin to tell Jesus what happened to you. Tell Jesus what they did to you. As you tell him, allow yourself to feel the emotions connected to the pain and release those painful emotions to Jesus. As you are releasing it, picture him taking it from you. Picture Jesus comforting you and covering you in that moment. Write down what you feel, hear, sense, or see Jesus doing.

- **Step 2**: Picture the person to whom the traumatic memory is connected to and say whatever comes up for you to tell them to release your emotions. After you finish, say their names, and tell them that you forgive them.

- **Step 3**: Picture yourself at the age where the trauma happened, and ask Jesus to come and heal your memory from the pain connected to the traumatic event. Picture Jesus healing you at the age where the trauma occurred. Write down what you feel, hear, sense, or see Jesus doing.

- **Step 4**: Say this prayer. *In Jesus's name, I repent, renounce, and release myself from any hurt, pain, anger, bitterness, hate, or any other feeling I am carrying connected to the trauma or the people that hurt me. In Jesus's name, I command healing to my mind, body, emotions, and spirit. I command every demonic spirit connected to this trauma and the people involved to come out of me now.*

- **Step 5**: Began to pray in your heavenly language and command the demonic spirits to come out of you in Jesus's name. As you are doing this, picture Jesus freeing you from every demonic spirit and filling you with his presence, joy, love, and strength.

Write down what you feel, hear, sense, or see is happening.

Note: If you need more support, please visit Godtherapy.net for an inner healing and deliverance counseling session.

We first talked about wounds in chapter 6, but here we are going to delve deeper. As a reminder, the three main areas where trauma causes wounds are:

1. Wounded Messages
2. Wounded Identity
3. Wounded Memory

THREE WAYS TO HEAL WOUNDED MESSAGES

1. **Identify the Unhealthy Message**

    The first step in healing wounded messages is identifying the damaging, negative, or unhealthy beliefs. Take some time and think about some unhealthy beliefs you carry about yourself and life and write them down.

2. **Challenge the Message**

    Now that you have identified them, the next step is to challenge them. You cannot just accept everything your mind tells you. It is important that you manage your mind and not allow your mind to control you. Remember your thoughts, drives your emotions which determines your behavior. If you want to be happy then you must think happy thoughts. It's okay to acknowledge the negative but you can't dwell on things. The quality of your thoughts determine the quality of your life.

As a Christian, it is your duty to evict these demonic wounded messages out of your mind and fortify your thoughts with the word of

God. A part of healing cognitive distortions is challenging the distortions. Here are some ways you can challenge wounded messages:

   a. Hearing what Jesus has to say about the message. This could look something like you closing your eyes and saying, "Jesus, I feel like I always fail. What do you have to say about that?" Then meditate on how Jesus would respond to you.
   b. Find a scripture to counter what the distortion is telling you.
   c. Get validation. Share your wounded message in a support group or with a loving supportive person who can affirm you.
   d. Use common sense thinking to challenge these distortions. If you feel like you always fail, think about the times where you did not fail. Pretend like the distorted message is on trial and you are the prosecutor. Your job is to gather evidence to prove the message wrong. Here are some questions you can ask yourself to provide the proof you need:
      - Where in my life has this proven not to be true?
      - Where in scripture do these messages contradict the word of God?
      - Take a deep breath, picture Jesus, and say, "Jesus, these are the wounded messages that I have been carrying. You said the truth shall make me free. What is the truth?" Write down what you hear, feel, sense, or think Jesus is saying.

3. **Replace the Unhealthy Message with a Healthy One**
   After challenging the messages, the next step is changing them. You can no longer speak or think the negative or unhealthy

message but commit to speaking and thinking healthy. Here is a prayer you can pray to free yourself from negative messages and commit to speaking positive.

Father God, I repent for speaking and thinking these messages (say what they are out loud). I realize that these messages go against your will and word. I submit myself to the truth of your word and declare these messages a lie. I break the power that these messages have on my mind, will, and emotions. Every curse that has been released in my life because of these messages, I break and replace them with blessings.

Father God, I commit to no longer speaking and believing these messages and I replace them with the word of God. In the name of Jesus, I command healing to every wound that is connected to these messages. In the name of Jesus, every demonic spirit that has entered because of these messages, I command you to come out of me immediately. Father, I pray that warrior angels be released right now to destroy and evict every demonic spirit connected to these messages in Jesus's Name.

WOUNDED IDENTITY AND HOW TO HEAL

Your identity is not how people see you, it is how you see yourself. Trauma has a way of tainting your self-perception. You develop a negative view of self. I have found that a lot of people who suffer from trauma do not like who they are. I assert why they do not like who they are because they do not know who they are. They are looking at themselves through the lens of what happened to them. This causes self-hate, self-rejection, low self-esteem, and a plethora of other diluted views of themselves.

You do not really know who you are until you get healed. The only way to honestly know who you are is to no longer see yourself through the scope of what happened to you. You must see yourself through the eyes of your Creator who created you to be like him.

> *"But as many as received him, to them gave he power to become the sons of God, even to them that believe on his name:" (St. John 1:12)*

> *"And God said, Let us make man in our image, after our likeness:" (Genesis 1:26)*

> *"Thank you for making me so wonderfully complex! Your workmanship is marvelous—how well I know it. You watched me as I was being formed in utter seclusion, as I was woven together in the dark of the womb. You saw me before I was born. Every day of my life was recorded in your book. Every moment was laid out before a single day had passed. How precious are your thoughts about me, Or How precious to me are your thoughts. O God. They cannot be numbered! I cannot even count them. they outnumber the grains of sand! And when I wake up, you are still with me!" (Psalm 139:14-18)*

Even before we were born, God has already predetermined our character and expresses his great love for us. Before you made that mistake that caused you to feel guilt and shame, Father God had already created you in his image and likeness. Before that thing happened to you to make you feel less than and impure, Father God created you in his image and likeness. It is in your DNA to be like God! The problem is if you do not know your identity, then you will not know your true character. Subsequently, instead of acting out of who God created you to be, you will act out of the trauma, not knowing that is not who you really are. Any way you act that is contrary to how God created you is not you. It may be how you behave, but it is not you. It may be who people say you are, but it is not you. Only your Creator has the power and the right to tell you who you are. You did not create yourself so you cannot tell yourself who you are. As a redeemed child of God, the Bible lets you know your true identity:

> *"But ye are a chosen generation, a royal priesthood, an holy nation, a peculiar people; that ye should shew forth the praises of him who hath called you out of darkness into his marvellous light: Which in time past were not a people, but are now the people of God: which had not obtained mercy, but now have obtained mercy." (1 Peter 2:9-10)*

> It is in your DNA to be like God!

A part of healing your identity is not accepting the negative messages about yourself. Not giving in to the stereotypes, verbal abuse, stigmas, or labels people place on you or that the devil will have you place on yourself. You must separate your actions from your identity. Your thoughts must be, *even though I did that, that is not me. Even though I had an abortion, or I am depressed or angry, this is not who I really am. This is not who God created me to be.* This will cause you not to settle and to work towards changing your actions and self-perception to line up with your godly identity.

Apostle Paul was a persecutor and murderer of Christians. For him to heal from guilt and be who God called him to be, he could no longer view himself through the mistakes of his past. He had to identify himself through the work of the cross.

> *"I am crucified with Christ: nevertheless I live; yet not I, but Christ liveth in me: and the life which I now live in the flesh I live by the faith of the Son of God, who loved me, and gave himself for me." (Galatians 2:20)*

> *"Therefore if any man be in Christ, he is a new creature: old things are passed away; behold, all things are become new." (2 Corinthians 5:17)*

God Encounters

Another part of healing your identity is having an encounter with Father God where he communicates to the fractured, confused, distorted, or abused parts of you and tells you who you are. The power of God's presence and voice is tangible and transformational. This is what happened to Gideon. He had a harmful view of himself due to the trouble he was experiencing in his life. He lived a life of fear and insecurity. The angel of God met him and told him his true identity:

> "And there came an angel of the Lord, and sat under an oak which was in Ophrah, that pertained unto Joash the Abi– ezrite: and his son Gideon threshed wheat by the winepress, to hide it from the Midianites. And the angel of the Lord appeared unto him, and said unto him, The Lord is with thee, thou mighty man of valour." (Judges 6:11-12)

Even though Gideon was acting weak, the angel of the Lord let him know that he was a mighty man of God. Even though Gideon was acting like a chicken, the angel let him know that there was an eagle inside of him. Gideon was the total opposite of what he thought and how he was behaving. Gideon's identity was so tattered that even though he had a supernatural encounter, he begins to question his calling and God's view of him.

> "And the Lord looked upon him, and said, Go in this thy might, and thou shalt save Israel from the hand of the Midianites: have not I sent thee? And he said unto him, Oh my Lord, wherewith shall I save Israel? behold, my family is poor in Manasseh, and I am the least in my father's house." (Judges 6:14-15)

For Gideon to be the leader God created him to be, he had to go through the process of God healing his identity. What was holding Gideon back was how he viewed himself. For the people to have the confidence to follow Gideon, Gideon had to develop confidence in himself. How you see yourself impacts your relationship with people. When you value yourself, you do not allow people to devalue you. When you know who you are, you can stand in boldness and not be intimidated by the opinions and critiques of man. Your self- confidence will allow you to soar and sit amongst dignitaries and not question whether you belong. Once Gideon's identity was healed, he was able to lead 300 people to defeat 300,000 Midianites! I wonder what God could do with you if you just believed in yourself and who God called you to be?

> *"And the Lord said unto Gideon, By the three hundred men that lapped will I save you, and deliver the Midianites into thine hand: and let all the other people go every man unto his place. So, the people took victuals in their hand, and their trumpets: and he sent all the rest of Israel every man unto his tent, and retained those three hundred men: and the host of Midian was beneath him in the valley." And the three companies blew the trumpets, and brake the pitchers, and held the lamps in their left hands, and the trumpets in their right hands to blow withal: and they cried, The sword of the Lord, and of Gideon. And they stood every man in his place round about the camp: and all the host ran, and cried, and fled. And the three hundred blew the trumpets, and the Lord set every man's sword against his fellow, even throughout all the host: and the host fled to Beth- shittah in Zererath, and to the border of Abel-meholah, unto Tabbath." (Judges 8: 7-8, 20-22)*

God is Speaking. Are You Listening?

Like any loving parent, God's desire is to speak to his children and restore how you see yourself. For that to happen, you must open your heart and allow God to speak to that fractured part of you at the age where the trauma occurred. The healing of your present self must take place at the age where the hurt first happened. You must ask yourself the tough questions, "Why don't I like myself and what caused it?" Then you must pray and ask God to show you who you are.

I have found that the more you seek God, the more he reveals himself to you. The more you know about God, the more you will know about yourself. The more confidence you have in God, the more confidence you will have in yourself. It is a trickle-down effect. You must seek your identity through God's word instead of what your fractured world is telling you. That is the key to building your character. When you realize who you are in Christ, you will refute those negative voices in your head that belittle you, and you will not allow demonic spirits to infiltrate your mind.

THE POWER OF HEALED MEMORY

After the traumatic memory is healed, you can talk about it without experiencing pain. That broken part of you that never had a voice can now be integrated into your core self so that you can be a whole person. With the memory healed, the pain from the past will no longer show up in your present. You can be free, get closure, and finally move on. You can experience the joy of this present life without it being interrupted by triggers from your past. You can walk in your true self without self-sabotaging due to the traumatic memories interfering with your emotions, decisions, and behaviors. Now your story can be used to help others that have traveled down the same road as you.

What once was an obstacle that you did not think you could overcome, now becomes a tool that God can use for his glory.

After they have been healed, I have had several clients go on to write books, establish ministries, travel to share their stories, and start businesses. When your memory is healed, it can be meaningful for you. What once was an obstacle that you did not think you could overcome, now becomes a tool that God can use for his glory. The Bible declares:

"And we know that all things work together for good to them that love God, to them who are the called according to his purpose." (Romans 8:28)

Though what happened to you was not a part of God's plan, he can use it for his purpose. Yes, God wants to use your pain for his purpose! Isn't that good news? There is always treasure in the trash that you have experienced in life. The reason why I decided to become a therapist was because of the pain that I have experienced. As I was navigating through depression, I felt like no one would understand me or help me. They would just tell me to pray about it or fast, and I did all that but still struggled. Through my pain, I developed a passion for learning how to help people heal and developed techniques and methods so that people can be made whole. After God healed me, I developed a compassion for the hurting, especially those who felt like no one understood or could help them.

Chapter 14

Keys to Healing from Your Past

You will never be able to fully move into your destiny until you heal from your history. Your future is waiting for you to be made whole. As human beings, we have the normal propensity to suppress our pain or try to forget the hurtful things that happened to us. When we do this, the pain sits in our subconscious and healing does not happen. To heal, you must do three things: face it, feel it, and forgive it.

FACE IT

The first thing we must do to heal is to face our issues head-on. To slay Goliath David had to run towards him. You will never get victory over your problem by acting like it didn't happen, trying to forget it, or covering it up. When you do this, things will never get better only worse. Your mental and emotional state will deteriorate and your ability to function in life will be debilitated by your unaddressed damage. Just like David used a rock and a sling shot to slay Goliath, you must tap into the resources around you as tools to help you to overcome the mental and emotional giants that's causing distress.

You Don't Have to Face the Person to Heal the Pain

Some people feel that in order to heal they must face the offender. The person that broke you is not usually the one that's going to fix you. On the contrary, this can worsen the wound.

Sometimes it is not wise to face the offender, especially if the trauma is severe and they have issues themselves. They may not even understand that they have caused you pain. Other times, the offender does not have the capacity, stability, or wisdom to support you around your healing. There are various ways you can address and heal your pain without facing the person. There is a process you can walk yourself through to address the person without speaking to a person. Here are some ways that you can take yourself through a curative process of facing your pain.

a. Write a letter to the person who hurt you expressing your feelings. Write what they did, how it affected you, and write whatever else you want to say to them. Allow yourself to feel, cry, be angry, etc. Decide to forgive them so that you can release what you have been holding on to. After you are done, you can throw away the letter, which symbolizes you releasing the trash from your past and moving forward. I recommend walking yourself through Step 2: "Removing Unforgiveness Healing Prayer Model," in my book God Therapy – 7 Step Guide to Inner Healing and Deliverance.

b. Get an empty chair, put it across from you, and picture the person who hurt you is seated in that chair. Say whatever you need to say and however you need to say it. This is all about releasing negative energy. Afterward, I recommend walking yourself through my Step 2: "Removing Unforgiveness Healing Prayer Model," in my book God Therapy.

c. Find a trusted friend, minister, or Christian counselor, and share your story of what happened. Allow yourself to experience and express the painful feelings. Afterward, you can have them walk you through the Step 2: "Removing Unforgiveness Prayer Model," in my book God Therapy.

d. Pray and express to God the pain that you are dealing with, what happened to you, or what the person did to you. Afterward, take some time to meditate and listen to what God has to say to you.

Prayer is not just you talking to God, it is God speaking to you.

When you follow these steps, I suggest you find a quiet, private environment where you can allow yourself to release the pain, rage, hurt, fear, etc. with no distractions. As the pain surfaces, take deep breaths and breathe into the pain.

FEEL IT

One of the worst things you can do is ignore, numb, or avoid your feelings. You cannot be whole if you do not feel it. You may not have been told this but feelings are meant to be felt. As a matter of fact, a part of the healing process is feeling. God created us with emotions and a part of releasing painful emotions is allowing yourself to feel them and express them. The more you release the emotions, eventually the emotional energy runs out and subsides. If handled properly, emotional triggers should not last more than thirty minutes. If it is mishandled, then it can be like adding water to a grease fire.

One of the things that make us human is our ability to feel. God created us to feel. When you become numb, you rob yourself of your humanity. Without the ability to feel, you become disconnected from self, others, and God. Just like you are not able to feel the pain, you are not able to feel joy, peace, and other positive emotions. This has an adverse effect on how you show up in the world.

When you do not adequately express your emotions, that painful energy is not released and stays in your body and compounds. So, instead of experiencing sadness, you become a sad person. What should have been short term becomes permanent.

I have had many sessions with people who have numbed

themselves. They have a flat disposition and rarely show any expression at all. I had a client that was sexually abused as a child and the only way she knew how to deal with it was to numb herself. Her body needed to dissociate from the pain to survive the harmful event as a child, but it no longer worked for her as an adult. She was emotionless. She came to me because her son was murdered, and she was not able to grieve. Her inability to grieve began to have an adverse impact on her behavior, memory, and work performance. She worked a six-figure job, made million-dollar deals, and was forgetting things and making mistakes that were impacting her clients. In due course, her job told her to take a leave of absence until she got the help she desperately needed.

> *. . . the more you allow yourself to feel and express your pain, the easier it is to heal the emotion, cast out demonic spirits, and then receive healing from the power of Jesus Christ.*

The suppressed, unaddressed pain began to build within her and manifest in other ways that were toxic. This was not just showing up at work. She explained that she was in and out of relationships because she could never become emotionally sensitive and affectionate to love someone. She had several men who proposed to her but never married because she would always sabotage the relationship by being disconnected and distant. Numbing became part of her everyday life. During the sessions, I walked her through her traumatic experiences to feel the emotions and allow herself to grieve, be angry, be sad, and whatever else came up. Slowly she began to reconnect with her feelings, allowing herself to grieve and be human again. When she could feel it, we could address it, and invite Jesus in to heal her hurt.

I have found that the more you allow yourself to feel and express your pain, the easier it is to heal the emotion, cast out demonic spirits, and then receive healing from the power of Jesus Christ. When you do not allow yourself to feel and choose to hide your pain instead, you are locking the pain and demonic spirits inside of you. You are also blocking the healing presence of God from entering that painful area.

FORGIVE IT

Forgiveness is one of the most important factors in the healing process. Some people feel that forgiving lets the person off the hook and they are not held accountable for what they have done. This is not true. Forgiveness does not mean that an individual should not face the consequences of their actions. It does not let the person off the hook, it lets *you* off the hook. When you do not forgive, you are hooked into the pain of what the person did. Forgiveness means that you are making a choice to no longer hold on to what the person did to you so that you can get unhooked. In other words, you release yourself from the emotional residue connected to what happened.

When you forgive, you are saying that you are letting go of all anger, bitterness, revenge, pain, sadness, fear, and any other emotion connected to what they did to you. *I am doing this, not because you deserve it, I am doing this because I deserve it. I owe it to myself to be free of what you did to me, and I cannot be free if I do not forgive.* When it comes to forgiveness, you cannot forgive any type of way you choose. There is a biblical way to forgive and an unbiblical way to forgive. For forgiveness to be effective, you must do it God's way. The Bible instructs you how to forgive.

"So likewise shall my heavenly Father do also unto you, if ye from your hearts forgive not every one his brother their trespasses." (Matthew 18:35)

To be free, you must forgive from your heart and not your head. You cannot be healed if you do not forgive from your heart.

Head Forgiveness vs Heart Forgiveness

Some people forgive religiously but they are not real. Head forgiveness is when you just say the words but do not really mean it from a heart level. When you forgive from your head, you disconnect yourself from the pain. This causes the pain to continue to be repressed. When you forgive from your head, the pain of what happened to you is still there, and the demonic spirits connected to what happened to you are there, too.

Forgiving from your heart opens the door for your healing and deliverance. The moment your heart is open and you forgive, the pain connected to the wound can surface, and you can invite Jesus to come in and heal the pain. Once healed, you can command any demon connected to the pain to be removed. If the pain is not experienced and released through heart forgiveness, demons can hide in the pain, and you will have difficulty getting them to leave. This makes deliverance difficult, and at times, impossible.

Forgiving from your heart allows you to release any ungodly feelings or attitudes you have developed because of what happened. As soon as you forgive from the heart you can release yourself from those damaging emotions that may be hiding in your heart. One of my clients who I was walking through inner healing had suppressed pain because of his

> Jesus longs and is eager to heal your pain so that you can experience the true freedom that comes through forgiveness.

mom. I had him picture his mother in front of him and say what he never had a chance to say. As he spoke to her from his heart, the issues, hidden emotions, and demons from his heart began to manifest. While expressing himself to his mother, he said to her, "I hate you!" He had no idea that was in his heart. What he was carrying in his subconscious manifested in his conscious. After he acknowledged that he was carrying hate for his mother, he made a conscious decision to forgive her, repent and renounce the hatred, and be healed.

When you forgive from your heart, you can acknowledge what's there and find closure so that you can move forward in your life. Jesus longs and is eager to heal your pain so that you can experience the true freedom that comes through forgiveness. Jesus doesn't want you to cover up your pain. Whatever you're feeling, he wants you to face it at the cross. Jesus invites us to bring our burdens to him so that he can heal them.

> *"Come unto me, all ye that labour and are heavy laden, and I will give you rest. Take my yoke upon you, and learn of me; for I am meek and lowly in heart: and ye shall find rest unto your souls." (Matthew 11:28)*

IT'S OKAY TO GET HELP

Every unpleasant thing that happens to us is not traumatic. Certain things can hurt you and the pain will quickly subside. Certain things can injure you, and with a bit of prayer and scripture reading, you can heal alone. Trauma can cause wounds to be so severe that you need assistance to recover. It requires help to heal.

I was walking around in the dark and hit my toe on the bed. The pain that went through my body had me leaping like a kangaroo. With a little screaming and rubbing my toe, the pain only lasted for about 5 minutes. In another incident, I was weightlifting, and the weights fell on my toe. Even though that was months ago, the damage was still there. No amount of screaming and rubbing could fix it. One of the reasons it is still there is that I neglected to go to the hospital to receive the proper treatment.

There is no need for you to suffer longer than you're supposed to simply because you're not getting the help that you need. As human beings, God has created us to need each other to survive and to heal. There is someone around you that God has equipped and called to help you overcome your challenge. They could be a therapist, psychiatrist, minister, pastor, or friend. Your responsibility is to find them and work with them to get the help you need. The book of Ruth talks about a woman named Naomi whose husband and two sons died. She suffered from grief, loneliness, and rejection. She felt that God had abandoned her, and her life was cursed. What she didn't realize was that God had strategically put Ruth in her life to be a blessing, a support and care for her. Ruth refused to leave her, and Naomi was able to recover through being connected to Ruth. It's imperative that you connect with the right people so that you can get cured.

Note: If you need more support, please visit Godtherapy.net for an inner healing and deliverance counseling session.

Chapter 15

Keys to Turning Your Pain into Purpose

Although God does not cause the traumatic pain in our lives, his desire is for you to use it for his glory and for his purpose. When you are free, healed, and whole, your focus should be how you can use your past as a tool to impact your present and future – how you can use your pain for a purpose to help those around you that are going through the same thing that you have come out of. The same energy and time you spent preoccupied with your pain, you can now spend working on your purpose. What the devil meant to harm you, God wants to use it to bless you and those around you. God loves making a fool out of the devil. His desire is for Satan's plans to backfire, making it a part of his divine purpose for you. If it did not destroy you, it will develop you.

Once healed, your goal should be to help others with their issues. Most businesses start as a solution to a problem. There is a TV show that I love to watch called *Shark Tank*. This is where inventors and creators stand before "sharks" or business investors, present their invention, and ask the sharks to invest in their business. What I realized is that a lot of the inventions and businesses were developed through the individual dealing with a crisis. There was no solution available for their crisis, so they created a solution and made it into a product. With tears in their eyes, some of them would share their journey of what they went through to get to the product they had created. It was their misery that caused them to make millions! Many of times I would look at what they created and wonder "Why didn't I think of that?" The reason I did not is because I did not go through what they went through. Most inventions, businesses, books, and ministries are birthed through problems and pain. You are not just going through just to go through, there is profit in your pain. The question is will you put in the time, energy, and resources to turn your pain into purpose.

Here are 7 keys to turning your pain into purpose:

1. **Find your Passion**: Sometimes, your pain can become your passion. What you did not like to talk about becomes a testimony for others to hear about and be impacted. One of the most powerful things you possess is your story. Within that story, there is passion because you are personally connected to it. No one can tell it like you because you're the one that experienced it. Your passion is what pushed you to fight through the trauma in your life and get the freedom you need. Usually, when you find your passion, you will find your purpose.

Your Passion is the Navigation System to Your Purpose

I thought I wanted to be a veterinarian because I liked animals. Notice, I did not say I was passionate about animals. Some people are passionate about animals, and they will fight you if you are cruel to animals. I was not passionate, but I thought they were fun. My parents would not allow us to have pets in the house so we would find stray dogs and cats and have them as our pets until we were caught and forced to let them go. One time we had a dog in the house, and my father came home from work. He was upstairs, and my brothers and I were downstairs trying to catch the dog and put him in the closet or something. The dog started barking. My father yelled, "Did I hear barking? The gig was up, and we had to let the dog go immediately. I think the longest we were able to hide a dog in the house was for a week, but we would always get caught.

So, when I turned sixteen, I decided to work at a veterinarian office, with the goal of becoming a veterinarian. My first day at work I was so excited. I could not wait to see the cute cats and adorable puppies. I could not wait to pet and play with the dogs. When I arrived, I was welcomed by the crazy sound of a multitude of dogs barking. My supervisor greeted me, handed me a bucket and rag, and walked me to small cages where the pets had defecated, and told me to clean them. The next day, they took me into a room where they kept the bigger cages for the large dogs like Rottweilers, German Shepherds, and Boxers. My job was to feed them. He gave me the food and left me alone. I walked up to one cage and saw this cute Rottweiler and decided that instead of feeding it through the cage, I was going to go into the cage, feed it, and pet it. Let's just say that I know God is real because I made it out of that cage alive.

The final straw for me was when I had to hold the animals while the veterinarian gave them their shots. There was this charming little kitten that I had to hold. As the needle was entering the kitten, the kitten managed to get a hold of my hand with its teeth. Now, I have been bitten by a dog, but there is nothing like being bitten by a kitten! The next day I quit. I believe I lasted two weeks. Being a veterinarian was not my passion nor my purpose, and to this day, I have no pets. I guess I am still traumatized by that kitten that bit me.

It was not until I was in undergraduate college that I found my passion. School was boring to me. In fact, it was torture. I hated sitting in class for long periods of time being lectured about a subject that I did not care for. I was simply going through the motions to earn my degree so I could make money working a nine to five job. Then I hit a turning point.

My major was business, but I decided to take a psychology class as an elective. I did not know what psychology was, but someone told me the class was easy, so I took it. The first day of class I reverted to my usual routine of sitting in the back, bored, daydreaming, and anxious for class to be over. While sitting in the back, slouched in my chair, I decided to open the book and read it.

Suddenly, it felt like I drank three bottles of Red Bull. As I began to read, something leaped inside of me. I went from being tired and bored to energized and excited. The answers that I was looking for to understand my struggles, mental issues, and emotional challenges were in this book. I realized that not only will this help me understand myself and how to address my issues, but I could also help others address their mental and emotional challenges. I finally found my passion which catapulted me into my purpose. I immediately switched my major to psychology, graduated and worked as a clinical therapist. I began to tap into my divine purpose and God gave the increase. Long story short, I opened my own Christian counseling practice, and currently conduct sessions weekly and train and coach licensed counselors and people in ministry.

My question to you: what are you passionate about? What do you love to do that you would do it for free? Now, think about how you can turn your passion into purpose. How can you reach your convergence? When you are doing something you love to do, you are good at it, and you are making money doing it, you have reached your convergence. This is when you are living life for a purpose and fulfilling your passion. Ask yourself, do you want to spend the rest of your life simply to pay bills and build someone else's dream or do you want to spend your life doing what you love and fulfilling your dreams and God's design for you?

2. **Turn Your Passion Into Purpose:** Think about how your passion can add value or meaning to other people. Think about what problem your passion solves. Think about how your passion can increase the quality of someone's life. When you have your answer, you have found your purpose. As you are thinking about it, pray about it. Ask God to reveal to you your purpose. I never knew that I would write a book and start my own inner healing and deliverance counseling practice. No one talked about trauma in church, and inner healing and deliverance were not a treatment model used in counseling. As I began to seek God about my passion, the Holy Spirit began to reveal to me how he wanted to use it for purpose. He began to give me visions, dreams, and encounters about inner healing and deliverance. He began to give me revelation about methods and steps so that people can heal from trauma and experience freedom. This was when I knew that my purpose and mission in life was to minister healing and deliverance to people. People thought something was wrong with me but I gave up my position as a salaried Sr. Pastor to pursue my purpose more specifically. As I was faithful and diligent in executing my passion and what I felt God gave me, he revealed to me the next steps. God gave me dreams and visions to show me my apostolic mission to train and equip his Church in the ministry of inner healing and deliverance. To use my skill, anointing, and calling to help the church address the trauma epidemic.

3. Turn Your Purpose into Products:

"Do not you realize that those who work in the temple get their meals from the offerings brought to the temple? And those who serve at the altar get a share of the sacrificial offerings. In the same way, the Lord ordered that those who preach the Good News should be supported by those who benefit from it." (1 Corinthians 9:13-14)

"Elders who do their work well should be respected and paid well, especially those who work hard at both preaching and teaching. For the Scripture says, "You must not muzzle an ox to keep it from eating as it treads out the grain." And in another place, 'Those who work deserve their pay!'" (1 Timothy 5: 17-18 NLT)

The scripture lets me know that God wants you to be supported by your purpose. Your business should be your ministry. Your career should be your calling. There is nothing wrong with monetizing your ministry. The more you monetize your ministry, the more you can build your ministry to have a more significant impact on people. The more you monetize your ministry, the more you can experience the blessings that come with ministry and be better able to take care of your family. Anything you do outside of your ministry to make "ends meet" takes time away from your ministry. When I say ministry, I am not speaking about preaching on a platform. Whether in the church or in the marketplace, anything you do that helps people is ministry.

There is nothing wrong with you making money doing ministry if your motive is not money. My father was a senior pastor and worked at the post office to take care of seven kids and a wife. I remember hearing him wake up at 4:00 a.m. in the morning getting ready for work ,and then I would see him come home at 3:00 p.m. I still remember the tired look on his face when he opened the door and took his hat off. He was so tired that falling asleep at the dinner table was the norm. He had a few moments to rest because he had to be at church for the 7:00 p.m. service.

Each Tuesday, he taught Bible study, Friday he preached for our Friday service, and Sunday was a full day— early morning Sunday school, Sunday morning service, evening Bible class, and Sunday night service. Oh, I did not mention him counseling people, dealing with problems that arose in the church, going to hospitals to visit the sick, preaching funerals, facilitating weddings, making home visits, and the list goes on and on. On top of that, he had a family to take care of. To say this was exhausting and overwhelming is an understatement.

Being a senior pastor myself, I understand the mental and emotional stress he was under. His job at the post office was taking away from his purpose of serving God's people and building the church. My father was a strong man that rarely showed emotion unless he was praising God. I never saw my father cry until he started pastoring. Eventually, he left the post office and became a salaried full-time pastor. This move was necessary. He was able to have the strength and time he needed to expand the church, lead outreach teams, win souls, pursue his vision to help the community, open a refuge house for recovering drug addicts, and so much more.

We can conclude from the scriptures above that it is God's will for you to profit from your purpose. I remember when God revealed to me the name *God Therapy* and how it would be a model that will bring inner healing and deliverance. My initial thought was just to use it for people in the church I was pastoring. Then the Holy Spirit woke me up and spoke clearly to me and said, "Mold, make, and monetize your ministry." This was when I had the vision to start a Christian counseling practice that would combine therapy, inner healing, and deliverance. Next, I decided to start *God Therapy Training Academy* to train Christians how to strategically and adequately walk someone through inner healing and deliverance and develop teams in their ministries and churches. All this would be at a fee. It is unfair for people to be served and not willing to sow. It is not fair for people to labor and others receive and not be willing to give. Paul said this to the Corinthians church:

> *"If we have sown unto your spiritual things, is it a great thing if we shall reap your carnal things?" (1 Corinthians 9:11)*

To turn your purpose into profit, you need to create a product. What products or services do you want to offer to others that is connected to your purpose? Maybe it's an online course. Maybe you are a motivational speaker. Maybe it's a blog where you sell your own and affiliate products. What do you want to sell that will continue to serve your purpose? The book that you are reading now is a product connected to my purpose.

4. **Develop Your Plan:**

> *"Let all things be done decently and in order." (1 Corinthians 14:40)*

This scripture is talking about structure. Zeal without structure is destructive. Put a plan behind your passion so you will not sabotage your purpose. Without structure, your dreams will self-destruct. Most businesses and ministries fail, not because it is not a good business or ministry, but because they have poor structure. Your bones are what gives your body structure and keeps everything in place. The purpose of your bones is for your body to be able to function without falling.

For your business or ministry to function without falling, you need to put certain organization and methods in place. You must write out a business or a ministry plan for your purpose. Next, develop a structure for how it will be organized and executed. You also need to establish short- and long-term objectives and goals. What do you want to accomplish this year, the next five years, and the next decade? Your success or failure is only a result of how you plan.

Zeal without structure is destructive.

I remember I decided to host my first conference. Before I did anything, I took a month to write out my plan from the location to the messages to the worship team, the marketing, and everything in between. I was prepared and even had contingencies just in case something went awry. I was shocked at the turn out. I was not a big name, nor did I have to bring in a popular person to fill the seats. The secret was that I planned, and everything was strategic. Some of us need to get delivered from a "last-minute" spirit. Take the time to develop your plan.

5. **Your Presentation:**

   Your Presentation Will Determine Your Elevation

   Your presentation is how you articulate to others what you do and what you offer. Have you ever noticed while driving down the street how some restaurants have pictures of their food displayed? The image of the food is not sloppy but is appealing to the eye. Food commercials are the same: the food looks fresh, juicy, and well put together. Even before you taste it, you are drawn to it. There have been several times where I was driving and saw a picture of food on a restaurant's window and made a U-turn to dine there.

This is because of the presentation. Your presentation is a representation of your product. It is more than just your appearance. Moreover, you are not just representing yourself but also the God that dwells in you. Do you dress like where you have been or where you are going? How do you want to brand yourself? A brand is more than a nice logo, website, and marketing materials. A brand constitutes every touchpoint a client has with you. Do you look disheveled and out of sorts? Are you dressed appropriately for your audience? Are you able to communicate who you are and your vision succinctly? Have you practiced your elevator speech? Are you nice or have a poor attitude? Are people naturally drawn to you because your light is shining brightly? Being mindful of these things can mean the difference between a mediocre business and product and one that soars. People come to me, not just because I am anointed, but because I am nice.

6. **Find Your People:** You need to find two types of people: those you are serving and those that will help you serve. You are not an island and cannot do it all by yourself. Even Jesus was not by himself. The first thing he did before he began his public ministry was choose his team. He found Peter, James, John, and nine other people and called them disciples to assist him with his purpose. Next, you must connect with people who are best served by your product. Do not expect them to find you, you must find them. Talk about your passion and business wherever you go.

I remember as a kid at prayer service in church, I would always hear the mothers praying and crying out to God, "Bring them in, Lord! Send them in, Lord!" These were powerful praying mothers, so I was puzzled by the fact that despite their fervent prayers, the people never came in the church. It wasn't until I was much older when I read a scripture that answered my bewilderment:

> *"And the lord said unto the servant, Go out into the highways and hedges, and compel them to come in, that my house may be filled."* (Luke 14:23)

Do not wait for them to come to you; you go to them. This is called networking, communicating, and going to the places where the people are that need your product. As soon as they see that you have what they need and you are an expert, they will purchase your product or services.

7. **Develop Your Platform:** The difference between good and great is not the product, it is the exposure. Some of the most anointed and gifted people I met were not on TBN or featured in Charisma magazine; they were at storefront churches. I do not believe this was God's will for them. I believe it was because they lacked the knowledge and skill to develop a platform. I remember when the Holy Spirit spoke to me about developing my platform. I thought he wanted to send me to other churches to teach and preach. I felt I needed to find a renowned public figure to announce what I do to get the exposure I needed. I was so excited, waiting for my phone to ring with some big name on the line saying they discovered me. The call never

came. Then God revealed to me that looking for someone to discover me was not my platform, that was someone else's platform. He wanted me to create my own platform and build my own brand. That way only he could get the glory out of my ministry and no one else could take the credit for what he gave me.

Instead of waiting for someone to call me to come to their conference, I created my own conference. As I began to obey God and develop my platform, people began to come to me. My phone began to ring and my schedule began to fill up because I developed a platform. I had something that people needed. I maxed out my Facebook page and had to create a business page so that more people could follow me. I began to go live online and teach about inner healing, deliverance, and therapy. I began to have virtual sessions and have had the privilege of ministering to people worldwide.

Please do not wait for someone to build a platform for you. God has called you and given you everything you need to establish your platform. It is not about being seen; it is about giving yourself the publicity you need to serve at a greater capacity. It's not about being popular, it's about fulfilling your purpose. When Jesus began his ministry, he did not hide. His first sermon was on a boat. Why did he preach his first sermon on a boat when the teachers of that time where teaching in the temple? Jesus wanted visibility. He wanted to get the people's attention so that they would follow him. As you read the following scripture, meditate on it from the viewpoint of developing your platform.

> *"Ye are the light of the world. A city that is set on a hill cannot be hid. Neither do men light a candle, and put it under a bushel, but on a candlestick; and it giveth light unto all that are in the house. Let your light so shine before men, that they may see your good works, and glorify your Father which is in heaven." (Matthew 5:14-16)*

The greater your platform, the greater your exposure. The greater your exposure, the greater your light will shine. The greater your light shines, the more God gets the glory.

For more information on private sessions or training courses, visit Godtherapy.net.

Chapter 16

From Misery to Ministry

Once God heals you, he wants to reveal you. St. John Chapter 4 talks about a Samaritan woman who came to a well where Jesus was to get something to drink. Normally, people came to the well at a particular time together, but the woman came to the well when she knew no one would be there. She came to the well in private because she was broken, embarrassed, ashamed, and wanted to hide. She had five husbands and the person she was currently with was not her husband. He probably was somebody else's husband. She did not want anybody to recognize her because of her history. On the outside, people saw a rachet, whorish woman. The women in the community gossiped and shunned her. The religious leaders condemned her and labeled her.

Let's take a look at her from a therapeutic lens. How people saw her on the outside was different from what was going on inside. I submit to you that she was acting out of her agony. On the inside, she was bruised and crying out for attention. She probably did not know what true love was, so she became acquainted with lust. Who knows what happened to her to cause her to go from man to man. Maybe her father wasn't in her life, and she was acting out of trauma. Perhaps she was molested as a girl and became pathologically promiscuous. Who knows? We know something happened to her, and now she's having an encounter with Jesus, the healer. She's thirsty, not for another man, but for the spiritual water that Jesus is offering that will fill the voids in her life.

> *"Jesus answered and said unto her, Whosoever drinketh of this water shall thirst again: But whosoever drinketh of the water that I shall give him shall never thirst; but the water that I shall give him shall be in him a well of water springing up into everlasting life. The woman saith unto him, Sir, give me this water, that I thirst not, neither come hither to draw." (John 4:13-15)*

No doubt the religious people tried to change her from the outside in, but her life was changed from the inside out after speaking to Jesus. Once transformed, she no longer wanted to be hidden. The shame, embarrassment, and trauma were immediately broken off her. That's the power of having one conversation with Jesus. She no longer wanted to be silent. She ran into the town and told everybody. The same men she flirted and slept with, she ministered to as a changed woman.

> *"The woman then left her waterpot, and went her way into the city, and saith to the men, Come, see a man, which told me all things that ever I did: is not this the Christ? Then they went out of the city, and came unto him." (John 4:28-30)*

This one woman brought the entire town to Jesus. A person that everyone thought was useless, God used to change the lives of hundreds. Imagine the hundreds, thousands, and even millions of souls that you can bring to Jesus through your ministry, through your message, through the business you birth from your deliverance. When your history no longer binds you, it's time to pursue your destiny. Once healed, the only thing that is holding you back is your failure to act. I pray and challenge you that as you conclude this book, not only do you receive your deliverance but that you passionately pursue your purpose. The best is yet to come. For more resources visit Godtherapy.net.

About the Author

Timothy Lane has worked as a clinical therapist for many years. He has an extensive background in individual, group and family counseling. He's worked as a clinical therapist for the Chicago Housing Authority, Chicago Public Schools, and the University of Chicago's psychiatric unit. Timothy has been involved in inner healing and deliverance for over fifteen years and has facilitated thousands of deliverance sessions.

He is the creator of *God Therapy*, a 7-step inner healing and deliverance model. He has a Christian counseling practice, and through his inner healing and deliverance model, he has seen people freed from some of the worst cases. He is also the founder of the *God Therapy Academy*, where he provides experiential training on his 7-step *God Therapy* model to bring deep-level inner healing and deliverance.

Timothy Lane is a third-generation pastor and served as a senior pastor for many years. He is currently serving as the Inner Healing & Deliverance Pastor for New Life Covenant S.E., a church with over 20,000 members. He is an influential teacher and speaker.

He is a person of compassion and love. He values family, is happily married, and is the father of 3 beautiful children. He holds a Master's degree in Counseling, B.A. in Psychology, and B.A. in Theology.

Made in the USA
Coppell, TX
20 May 2025